THE NATURAL, SUGARLESS DESSERT COOKBOOK

THE NATURAL SUGARLESS DESSERT COOKBOOK

Carole Collier

WALKER AND COMPANY
NEW YORK, NEW YORK

First published in the United States of America
in 1980 by the Walker Publishing Company, Inc.
Published simultaneously in Canada by Beaverbooks,
Limited, Pickering, Ontario.

ISBN: 0-8027-0647-9
Paper ISBN: 0-8027-7161-0

Library of Congress Catalog Card Number: 79-91252

Printed in the United States of America

Book designed by Robert Barto

10 9 8 7 6 5 4 3 2

For the Weber family

Contents

Introduction

TRADITIONALLY, exciting desserts are lavish concoctions rich in sugar and unwanted calories. As a health-minded public, we know we should avoid them, yet we want them and often give in to our craving for sweets. According to U.S. Department of Agriculture statistics, an average American consumes almost two pounds of white sugar a week, plus one more pound of sugar in other forms —honey, corn syrup, maple syrup, etc. Three fourths of the sugar we eat comes in processed foods. These figures show just how much we depend on sugar. Meanwhile, sugar and sugar substitutes remain the center of much controversy.

Scientific studies, although not conclusive, seem to show some evidence that sugar is directly linked to heart attacks, increased blood lipids, cholesterol and triglyceride levels. Without a doubt, it is directly linked with the development of obesity in many cases; and obesity brings a greater risk of heart disease, diabetes and a variety of other disorders. Additionally, high sugar intake is a major factor in causing tooth decay.

Refined sugar is a processed, highly concentrated food that has been stripped of its fiber and valuable nutrients. While it contributes nothing but unwanted calories, it requires vitamins in order to be digested. When large amounts of refined sugar are consumed, the body's store of vitamins is depleted. These vitamins are robbed from nerves, muscles, skin, blood and organs. Having the body thus drained of its stored nutrients leaves it exposed to a multitude of disorders. Nervousness, fatigue, digestive disorders, gum disease and skin problems have all been attributed to high sugar intake.

Other sugars are really no better; they cause the same reaction in the body. Although white sugar, brown sugar, raw sugar and molasses are classed as "nutritive sugars," do not be misled. They are called "nutritive" only because the body is able to use their calories for energy. They contain only a few minerals in minute amounts, and it is unnecessary to take on a big load of calories to obtain any of these, especially when the calories are not accompanied by a significant quantity of any vitamin. More often than not, these other sugars are white sugar in disguise: brown sugar is "man-made" by combining table sugar with caramel coloring; turbinado is table sugar with a bit of molasses left in; Demerara is also table sugar with a bit of molasses. Raw sugar is table sugar with cane fiber or beet pulp added to mime the taste of authentic raw sugar, which is too impure to sell commercially. Fructose is a natural sugar, but in its granulated state it is highly refined and stripped of nutrients. Honey, molasses and maple syrup do contain some vitamins, but again the amounts are so insignificant that excess use of these sweets does more harm than good. They should always be used in moderation.

Saccharin's popularity is an indication of the public's awareness of the dangers of high sugar intake. However, it too is suspected of being harmful. Saccharin is a product of coal tar; sulfuric acid and other chemicals are used to manufacture it. Studies showing that it can cause bladder cancer in test animals are not conclusive, but they do raise questions about possible long-term, heavy-use effects. There is also a Canadian study divulging a 60% higher incidence of bladder cancer in males who consume saccharin than in those who do not. As well as being artificial, saccharin is another sweetener providing no vitamins, so that it, too, places a strain on our body's natural store. It's classed as non-nutritive because it contains no calories. Because it is not a food and there is a risk, we should certainly avoid using it. Moreover, it leaves an unpleasant aftertaste, which many people cannot become accustomed to.

Since the need and demand for sweets is so prevalent in our society, what then is the answer? An obvious solution lies in utilizing sweet fruits that contain healthful vitamins, minerals and fibers, as well as natural sugars. Simply put, in the normal diet one should substitute for sugars by eating fruits that are rich in nutrients and that will, at the same time, satisfy the craving for sweets.

Everyone is aware of what a wholesome food fruit can be. Natural sugar, as it occurs in fruit, is accompanied by the full assortment of vitamins and minerals necessary for the assimilation and use of that sugar by the body. Since fruits are mostly water, their caloric content is generally low. They are also very low in fat and contain no cholesterol, and they are usually low to very low in sodium. In addition, the fiber in fruit (and vegetables), particularly pectin, which is found in varying amounts in all fruits, is currently being studied for possible benefits. Dietary fibers found in food consist of cellulose, hemicelluloses, lignin, pectins and gums. Scientists and doctors are still learning about dietary fiber, but some tests have indicated the possibility that it may protect against cancer of the colon, ischemic heart disease (obstruction of coronary arteries), appendicitis and diverticular disease (pockets in the wall of the colon that fill with stagnant material and become inflamed).

Although fruit can be very beneficial, it is not so for everyone. It may offer some protection against various diseases, but it is not a cure. Persons already afflicted with unbalanced blood-sugar levels—diabetics and hypoglycemics—are usually placed on restricted diets and may have been advised to avoid specific fruits, among other foods. In such cases, they should check with their doctor before using various forms of fruit as a substitute for sugar. It is interesting to note that research is currently being done on fructose (fruit sugar) as a benefit to diabetics, because it does not require insulin to carry it to the body's cells. However, since studies are incomplete, diabetics should not use fructose without first consulting a physician.

Fruit and cheese is, of course, the classic finale to a fine meal. But, although there is an abundant variety of both products, one can still easily grow tired of such a simple dessert. Fortunately, fruits are available in many forms—fresh, frozen, dried, canned, juices, concentrates and wines. With a bit of imagination, it is possible to create a variety of more exciting desserts by substituting these naturally sweet fruit forms for sugar. The purpose of this book is to help you learn how to use fruits to their maximum capacity as the only sweetener in all your desserts. The recipes make use of unsugared concentrated fruit juices, fruit concentrates, and those wines that do not contain added sugar, as well as the fruit itself, to create an enticing variety of naturally sweet desserts.

Fruits

FRESH FRUIT

THROUGH modern farming practices, efficient methods of handling and storing, and rapid transportation, we are fortunate to have an abundant variety of fresh fruits available all through the year. Yet, with such a vast amount to choose from, the quality can vary widely. In order to avoid using additional sugar with fruit, you must learn how to select the best, that which has the most sweetness and flavor. This can be done by keeping in mind a few simple rules when shopping:

Finding a reliable produce dealer is very important. Farm stands and orchards, fresh produce stores, and supermarkets should be chosen in that order for the best quality fruit available.

When buying small fruits such as berries or grapes, taste one before making your selection to make sure the fruit is as sweet as you expect it to be. Most dealers won't mind your tasting as long as you don't eat your way through their store. If they're proud of the produce they have to offer, they may even cut an orange or an apple for you to sample.

Make an effort to purchase fresh fruits when they are in season, and preferably at their peak. This will not only insure maximum ripeness, but will also give an added bonus of good economy. Remember the times you paid a fortune for the first fruit of the season (strawberries come to mind) and then were let down because they required a hefty sprinkling of sugar? A calendar guide to the fruit seasons is available on pages 146-147.

Plant-ripened fruit should be your first choice. As fruit ripens naturally, its sugar content increases through the growing process of the plant and from the bathing rays of the sun; it becomes soft, juicy and sweet. With the exception of bananas and pears, fruits will taste best if they are allowed to ripen on the plant. Grapes, pineapples, melons and berries are examples that can be pretty tasteless if picked before they are matured. If you have your own garden or live near a fruit farm or orchard, you are in an ideal position to obtain naturally ripened fruits in their prime. If not, vine-ripened produce is usually advertised as such; look for the posted information.

Agricultural grading standards based on size, color, maturity and lack of defects are used voluntarily by fruit producers. U.S. Extra Fancy, U.S. Fancy, and U.S. 1 are the best grades to look for.

Since most ripe fruit deteriorates rapidly, however, it is usually picked before prime. When unripe fruits are to be harvested early, they must be mature enough to have developed their maximum potential of sugar; they may then be ripened artificially or at home and still retain a goodly portion of their sweetness. Such fruit will never be quite as delicious as naturally ripened fruit, but the flavor and texture should be acceptable. Immature fruit, picked early and then ripened artificially, may be soft and juicy, but it will lack the flavor of naturally ripened or mature ripened fruit because it will lack the sugar. This is often the case when peaches, apricots and nectarines are sold with a greenish tinge not common to their variety; no matter how carefully you choose and ripen the fruit, it's bound to be insipid. The total sugar content does not develop properly unless the fruit has been matured on the plant. How can you tell if unripe fruit is mature or immature? Immature fruit is rock-hard, underdeveloped, and usually has a greenish background color; mature fruit should yield just slightly under pressure, be of good varietal proportions, with fully developed color. This is not always the case, however, and sometimes the appearance of fruit can be deceptive. Becoming familiar with each fruit's desirable characteristics should be of more help when making your judgments. There is detailed information on individual fruits on the following pages.

Of course, some fruits are not as sweet as others; for our purpose it is necessary to concentrate only on those that may contain enough sweetness to be used without additional sugar. Sour or tart types of fruit such as lemons, limes, some apples, etc., have been intentionally omitted.

FROZEN FRUITS

Unfortunately, most fruits must be packed in a sugar syrup in order to be frozen successfully. With the exception of whole small berries, which may be dry-packed, and certain other fruits specified in the recipe section of this book, we must, therefore, for our purposes here, avoid frozen fruit. Freezing also dulls the flavor and sweetness of fruit. If, in an emergency, you must resort to using frozen dry-pack fruit, here are a few tips:

When buying frozen dry-pack berries, make sure that the fruit makes a rattling sound when you shake the package.

If the container is transparent, take note of the color of the fruit; brighter color indicates fresher flavor.

Always read the label to make sure that sugar has not been added.

Frozen fruit juice concentrates are another story altogether, and are discussed in the Fruit Juice section.

DRIED FRUITS

These are the candies of the fruit world. As the water is removed from the fruit, the sugar becomes concentrated, making them a wonderful source of natural sweetness, available throughout the year. Fruit may be sun dried, or dried in dehydrators. Sun-dried fruit, labeled as such on the package, should be your first choice. It contains slightly more moisture than dehydrated fruit and thus has a more desirable texture. In addition, sun-dried fruits are usually of higher quality and better flavor.

Dried fruit may also be either sulfured or unsulfured. The sulfur dioxide is often listed as a preservative when ingredients are labeled on a package. The sulfur also kills any pests or bacteria that might attack the sweet fruit. Although its use is considered beneficial by the industry, some questions have arisen about its effect on health. Unsulfured fruits are generally available in health-food or specialty stores. Regarding flavor, unless a manufacturer has been unduly heavy-handed with the use of sulfur, it is difficult to detect its presence in dried fruit. The air we breathe today, especially in the larger cities, has become so polluted and contaminated that we no longer notice many odious smells and flavors. Sulfur dioxide is one of the major air pollutants, and most of us are accustomed to breathing it. The next time you pass a specialty store that sells dried fruit in bulk, you may wish to experiment by contrasting a sulfured and an unsulfured peach or apricot. They are often sold side by side, with the unsulfured being slightly more expensive. Expect to pay for your samples, as dried fruit is costly and no free tastes are allowed, as might be the case when buying grapes or cherries. Most prepackaged dried fruits are sulfured; bulk fruit is sold both sulfured and unsulfured.

Aside from reading labels to see how fruit was dried or if it contains sulfur, the packaging itself is a good indication of quality. Dried fruits sold in bulk, or in transparent bags or plastic boxes, are on display for your inspection. Fruit should be plump and of good color and size. Avoid pale or dried-out-looking specimens. Fruit packaged in paper-wrapped or cardboard boxes may be hidden from view for a good reason. My advice is to trust your eyes, and don't buy what you can't see.

All dried fruit should be stored covered or tightly sealed in a cool, dark place and preferably in the refrigerator if it is to be kept for any length of time.

Just about any kind of fruit can be dried, but dates bear a special mention. They are sold both fresh (pressed) and dried, but it is often difficult to tell what they are from their appearance; the two types look similar. Fresh (pressed) dates are usually sold in bulk while dried dates are sold in cardboard or plastic containers. Beware of the dried fruit and read the label carefully, as it may have corn syrup added to make the fruit look more attractive. It may also have been pasteurized to prevent molding. Pressed dates store just as well as dried in the refrigerator and are definitely the preferred fruit to buy.

Home drying of fruits and vegetables is relatively easy and has seen a revival in this country. There are home drying kits on the market that can be used for either oven or sun drying, and there are also ready-made electric food dehydrators. Plans for building a portable electric food dehydrator are detailed in *Agriculture Idea Sheet No. 40.* A single copy will be sent free on request from Agricultural Engineering, Cornell University, Ithaca, N.Y. 14853. Details and a few recipes for home drying are available in *Information Bulletin 120* of the Cornell extension service. Send 40 cents to The Division of Nutritional Sciences, State Colleges of the State University, Cornell University, Ithaca, N.Y. 14853.

CANNED FRUITS

It is most important to read the label when selecting a can or jar of fruit. Fruits that are packed in light or heavy syrup always contain added sugar. "Packed in Natural Juice," "Water Packed," "No Sugar Added," and "Unsweetened" are the words to look for on a label in order to avoid added sweeteners. In the special diet section of the supermarket, you may also find fruits packed in juice from concentrates. More and more manufacturers are using fruit concentrates to increase the sweetness of their products, as the demand for natural products increases. Although they don't compare to fresh fruits in quality or flavor, it's not a bad idea to keep one or two cans of fruit in your cupboard for the unexpected emergency. They can be dressed up by serving them with ice cream, topping them with a sauce, briefly stewing or baking them with wine, or substituting them for fresh fruits in recipes calling for cooked purées or those that require only short cooking time. Canned unsweetened applesauce, of course, is a great time-saver and has come to the rescue more than once. If you only require a small amount of fruit purée, jars of unsweetened baby food come in very handy.

Fruit
Juices

A HUGE variety of processed fruit juice is available, in several forms: canned, bottled, cartoned, and as frozen concentrate. Again, it is necessary to read the label and look for the words "natural," "unsweetened," or "no sugar added." And never assume that because a product is unsweetened in one form, it remains unsweetened in another; bottled grape juice may be found unsweetened in red, white and purple varieties, yet frozen grape juice concentrate is usually sweetened. Some juices, although they are unsweetened, contain enough natural sugar so that they, themselves, can be used as a sweetening ingredient in many recipes. Unsweetened apple, grape, orange, orange-pineapple and pineapple are among those that are not at all difficult to find. Most nectars, however, including pear, peach, apricot, papaya, etc., usually contain added sugar.

The sweetest juices that contain no added sugar are, of course, those in frozen juice concentrate form. About three fourths of the water has been removed from the whole juice, leaving a product with most of its nutrients, flavor and natural sugar condensed into a small amount of liquid. As such, frozen juice concentrates, when thawed but not diluted, make a very useful sweetening ingredient. Experiment with using them in your tea as well. When reading recipe ingredients, be careful not to confuse juice concentrates with fruit concentrates. They are two entirely different products. Fruit concentrates are discussed in detail in the following section.

Those of you who are opposed to consuming wine may find unsweetened grape juice an appropriate substitute in many recipes.

Fruit
Concentrates

FRUIT concentrates (not to be confused with juice concentrates) are generally made from the whole fruit, including skins, seeds and core, or as much of the whole fruit as possible. They are high in fructose (fruit sugar) and pectin, and have a somewhat thicker consistency than frozen juice concentrates. This thicker texture closely resembles that of honey and makes fruit concentrates a good substitute when one feels the need for a change. In addition, they are available in a large assortment of flavors (all natural), listed here in order of sweetness. The first is the sweetest, and in this case, the last is least: grape, apple, black cherry, blackberry, apricot, peach, red raspberry, strawberry, cranberry.

To make fruit concentrate, the fruit is heated at a very low temperature. Most of its water is extracted, and the only thing remaining is concentrated solids. They require refrigeration only after opening.

Many manufacturers of diet foods are turning to fruit concentrates as the sole source of sweetening for their products. If you read the labels on some of the dietetic products available in the supermarkets, especially the canned fruits, you will notice this trend. Actually the fruit concentrates are only slightly lower in calories, ounce per ounce, depending on the flavor used, than refined sugar. But, because fructose (fruit sugar) has more sweetening power than sucrose (refined sugar), less is usually needed.

Aside from experimenting with fruit concentrates as a sweetener in recipes, you might find them delightful just poured over yogurt or ice cream as a topping or added to your tea as a beneficial sugar substitute.

Fruit concentrates are only sold in natural-food or health-food stores. However, if stores near you do not carry them, you can order them by mail from the following manufacturers: (Write first for a price list and postage and handling fees) Bernard Jensen Products, P.O. Box 8, Solana Beach, CA 92075 (grape, apple, and black cherry only); Hain Pure Food Co., Inc., P.O. Box 54841 Terminal Annex, Los Angeles, CA 90054.

Honey

In a sense, honey can be considered a fruit product since it is made by bees that have repeatedly gathered their pollen from the flowers of fruit trees. Of all the traditional sweeteners mentioned on page x, honey is by far the preferred. Indeed, many health-conscious people advocate its use as a sweetener, and many recipes have been published using it as a sweetening ingredient. The problem with honey, however, is that it has a very distinct flavor. The lighter-colored honeys have a less pronounced flavor than the darker ones, but it still often predominates in the finished product.

If you desire, honey may be substituted in equal amounts in any of the recipes in this book that call for the use of *fruit* concentrates (not to be confused with *juice* concentrates). The texture of honey is slightly thicker than that of fruit concentrates, but the difference is minimal and will not spoil any recipe. An excellent source of recipes that use honey as the sole sweetening agent is *Rodale's Naturally Delicious Desserts And Snacks*, by Faye Martin, published by Rodale Press.

Wines

WINES have a gala quality and are often used to create culinary delights for special occasions. Many are sweet or medium-dry (medium-sweet) and can be used in place of sugar or artificial sweeteners in making festive desserts.

Wine is the naturally fermented juice of ripe grapes. It is considered a food because it contains small amounts of vitamins A, B and C and at least thirteen valuable minerals. Depending on its richness, one ounce of wine will furnish approximately 18 to 43 calories.

The calories in sweet wines come both from the alcohol content and the residual sugar content (explained below). When these wines are cooked, the alcohol in them evaporates and so do the calories contained in the alcohol; the only calories remaining are those from the sugar (the natural grape sugar, in this case). Anyone who is especially worried about consuming alcohol or additional calories should find cooking with wines a delicious benefit.

Table wines are those which have an alcohol content between 7% and 14%. Most of the sweeter wines in this category are white. The majority of the sweet and medium-dry table wines are made from grapes which have a naturally high sugar content due to the variety and to good weather conditions during growing. As the sugar in the fruit ferments, it is converted into alcohol by natural yeasts. When the desired 7% to 14% alcohol level is reached, the fermentation is stopped and the wine is then left with an amount of residual sugar which has not been converted into alcohol. The higher the residual sugar content, the sweeter the wine. Table wines that are labeled "Late Harvest" or "Late Picked" are usually the sweetest of these because the grapes have received the maximum exposure to the sun. In Germany these wines are labeled *Spätlese, Auslese, and Beerenauslese*; the last being the sweetest.

It is interesting to note that sometimes the grapes used in winemaking, due to bad weather conditions and lack of sunshine, do not contain enough sugar naturally to produce the required amount of alcohol. Additional sugar must then be added to the juice before or during fermentation. This is called "chaptalisation." France and Germany, to some extent, are allowed by law to do this, but only when necessary. In many other countries it is forbidden. Even so, this additional sugar is always completely converted into alcohol and, therefore, there is no need to disregard this wine. An alternative solution to sugaring a wine is to add evaporated must (the mash of grape juice, pulp and skins from which wine is made) or concentrated grape juice. This method is used in countries where adding sugar is forbidden. Like other fruit concentrates, evaporated must is a natural fruit product and as such, its use in a wine will not disqualify that wine in sugarless cookery.

Other naturally sweet table wines are produced by leaving the grapes on the vine until a special mold named *Botrytis cinerea* or "noble rot" settles upon them. The grapes, however, are not rotten; they are simply overripe. In this condition, their skins become perforated and the water content of the grape evaporates. This causes the fruit to shrivel and concentrates the sugar. Wine of this type is always rich and sweet. Barsac and Sauternes from France are examples of those which can sometimes be found at a reasonable price. American Sauterne is *not* made in this way, although some American wines labeled "Botrytised," "Late Harvest," or "Late Picked" may be, if the climatic conditions are suitable. This type of wine is usually sold in a clear bottle; as a rule of thumb, providing the wine is healthy, the more golden a wine, the richer its flavor will be.

Fortified wines are those which have been strengthened during or after fermentation by the addition of grape alcohol, so that their alcohol content is increased to between 14% and 24%. The use of the term "fortified" is not allowed in the United States and such wines are usually called "dessert wines." Some examples are sherry, Porto (Portugal), port (United States), Madeira and Marsala. Some of these wines have evaporated must or grape-juice concentrate added to increase their sweetness and flavor. They do not, however, have any added sugar. This is surprising because many of them are so lusciously sweet.

Unfortunately, there are some wines that do have sugar added in order to increase their sweetness. Following the recipe section is additional information to aid you in selecting only those wines that are naturally sweet. Of course, it is not possible to cite every wine nor every country where wines are produced, but those that are mentioned are generally available throughout the United States. Remember, too, that stores selling wine have limited space and might not stock the specific wine you'd like to buy. Do not pass a store by because of its shortage of space; most reputable dealers are anxious to be helpful and will usually place a special order at no additional charge. If you don't see the wine that you want, ask if they will order it for you, even if it's only one bottle.

LONGEVITY OF WINE

Wine, like fruit, is a perishable item. Unopened, it should be stored horizontally in a cool, dark place, free of humidity and vibration. Once the bottle is opened, it begins to deteriorate, sometimes rapidly, and should be consumed as soon as possible. When using a specific sweet table wine in a recipe, try to serve the remainder of the bottle with the dessert course or as an after-dinner drink. If this is not possible, taste the wine shortly after opening it or before you put it away so that you will be able to test its flavor before using it at a later date. If a wine in the table category is to be saved, pour the unused portion into a smaller bottle so that there is as little air space at the top as possible; cover it tightly or recork it and refrigerate. Most table wines handled this way will keep nicely for one or two weeks, sometimes longer. Fortified (dessert) wines do not require refrigeration, but should be stored in a cool, dark place. Opened, they will keep for several months and sometimes years. Always remember to handle your wines gently and never shake them.

VINTAGES

SOMETIMES a bottle of wine will have a vintage date printed on the label. This date signifies the year when the grapes used in the wine were harvested. Most people become unduly concerned when it comes to vintage dates and vintage charts. Both good and not-so-good wines are produced in every year, even in the best years. Therefore, a vintage date on a wine bottle does not necessarily mean that the wine is of exceptional quality.

Wines that are blended from several grape varieties usually do not have a vintage date, because the grapes may have been harvested at different times. Many of the fortified and dessert wines fall into this category. If you don't see a vintage date on the bottle, it is no cause for alarm.

Tasting a wine, no matter what the vintage year, is the only way to tell whether or not you will like it. Should you have a choice of different vintages when making a selection, you may wish to bear the following in mind:

A higher price might (but not necessarily) indicate a better quality.

Light, white table wines are meant to be drunk young; choose a vintage not more than 3 years old. Sauternes, Barsac and other late-harvest wines are exceptions and can often improve with some aging.

Recipes

None of the following recipes contains any added refined sugar, artificial sweetener, honey, molasses or corn syrup. Yet every recipe is for a truly delectable dessert with a generous amount of sweetness. Fruit, in one form or another, is the sole sweetening ingredient used.

Many of the recipes are adapted from old-time favorites that will delight your family and friends; others are gorgeous creations suitable for the most elegant occasion. No matter how elegant they appear to be, they are all fairly easy to prepare.

The metric measurements appear in brackets, following the usual American Standard measurements. The American Standard and the metric measures, however, are not exact equivalents. In order to avoid the use of lengthy decimals, we have rounded out the metric, so be sure to work with either one set of figures or the other. It is hoped that you will enjoy and use this book long after the American Standard has disappeared.

Frozen Desserts

Grape Drops

The flavor of grapes intensifies when they are frozen. Frozen grapes make a delectable, literally melt-in-your-mouth substitute for candy. Simply wash and stem a bunch of green seedless grapes and dry them on paper toweling. Space them on a cookie sheet or in a dish and place in your freezer until they are hard. Then transfer them to a plastic bag and store in the freezer. Suck or crunch while frozen.

Persimmon Dessert Ice

Allow 1 persimmon per person. Wash persimmons and pat dry with paper towels. Space them on a cookie sheet or in a dish and place in the freezer until hard. Allow them to defrost partially for about 15 minutes before serving. Served partly frozen, they make a wonderful sort of natural sherbet.

Banana Chips

Select firm, semiripe bananas; peel and cut into 1-inch (2.5-cm) slices. Space them on a cookie sheet and freeze. Transfer them to a plastic bag and store in the freezer to be used as a snack. The texture of frozen bananas is similar to ice cream.

Banana Ice Cream

3 or 4 large ripe bananas
¾ cup (175 ml) heavy cream, whipped

Set freezer thermostat control to quick freeze. Peel the bananas, wrap in freezer paper, and freeze until firm. Mash the frozen bananas—there should be about 3 cups (750 ml)—and fold them into the whipped cream. Transfer the mixture to a 1-quart (1-liter) freezer container, seal tightly, and freeze until firm. Any flavor of fruit concentrate may be used as a topping, if desired. The ice cream may also be sprinkled with chopped nuts.

Serves 6

Orange-Pineapple Frozen Yogurt

2 cups (450 g) plain yogurt
6 ounces (175 ml) frozen unsweetened
orange-pineapple juice concentrate, thawed

In a mixing bowl, beat the juice concentrate with the yogurt until blended. Transfer mixture to a freezer tray, and freeze, stirring occasionally, for about 1 hour, until almost firm. Turn the partly frozen mixture into a large bowl, break up any lumps with a fork, and beat with a rotary beater or an electric mixer until smooth. The mixture should be slushy, but not melted. Return the mixture to the freezer tray and cover the surface with foil or plastic wrap to prevent ice crystals from forming; freeze until firm. Allow to stand at room temperature for 10 minutes before serving.

Yield: 3 cups (750 ml)

Papaya Stuffed with Tropical Sherbet

2 cups (500 ml) unsweetened pineapple juice
6 ounces (175 ml) frozen unsweetened orange juice
* concentrate*
2 medium-size bananas
4 ripe papayas
3 tablespoons (45 ml) shredded unsweetened coconut
* (fresh or available packaged at health-food stores)*

Place the first 3 ingredients in a blender container and process until smooth. Pour mixture into a large ice-cube tray and freeze, stirring occasionally, for 45 minutes to 1 hour, until almost firm. Turn the partly frozen mixture into a large bowl, break up any lumps with a fork, and beat with a rotary beater or an electric mixer until smooth. The mixture should be slushy, but not melted. Return the mixture to the ice-cube tray or a 1-quart (1-liter) plastic container and cover the surface with plastic wrap to prevent ice crystals from forming; freeze until firm. Allow to stand at room temperature for 15 minutes before serving.

Halve the papayas and remove the seeds. Place a scoop of sherbet in each cavity and sprinkle with shredded coconut.

Serves 8

Pineapple-Date Ice Cream

1 cup (250 ml) half-and-half
½ cup (125 ml) chopped, pitted pressed dates
½ banana, peeled
8 ounces (225 g) canned unsweetened crushed
    pineapple

Pour ½ cup (125 ml) of half-and-half into a blender container; add the dates and process until fairly smooth. Add the banana and process until blended. In a large mixing bowl, add the remaining ½ cup (125 ml) of half-and-half to the crushed pineapple; stir in the blended ingredients. Transfer to a freezer tray, cover the surface with foil or plastic wrap, and freeze until firm.

Serves 4

Ported Strawberry Ice Cream

1 teaspoon (5 ml) unflavored gelatin
½ cup (125 ml) ruby port
2 cups (500 ml) crushed fresh strawberries
¾ cup (175 ml) heavy cream

Sprinkle the gelatin over the port in a heat-resistant cup and let stand for 5 minutes to soften. Set the cup in a pan of very hot water, and gently stir until gelatin is dissolved. Use a rubber spatula to scrape the dissolved gelatin into the strawberries; mix well. Turn strawberry mixture into a freezer tray and freeze, stirring occasionally, for about 1 hour, until almost firm.

Beat the heavy cream until it stands in peaks. Turn the partly frozen strawberry mixture into a large bowl, break up any lumps with a fork, and beat with a rotary beater or electric mixer until slushy, but not melted. Fold in the whipped cream.

Return the mixture to the freezer tray and cover the surface with foil or plastic wrap; freeze until firm. Allow to stand at room temperature for 5 minutes before serving.

Yield: 1 quart (1 liter)

Frozen Zabaglione with Chocolate Sauce

6 egg yolks
2 tablespoons (30 ml) frozen unsweetened orange
juice concentrate, thawed
⅓ cup (90 ml) sweet Marsala or Florio Almond Cream
Marsala
1½ cups (350 ml) heavy cream
Chocolate Sauce (page 69)

Set freezer thermostat control to lowest setting. Place six 9-ounce (275-ml) wineglasses or goblets in the refrigerator to chill.

In the top part of a double boiler, beat the egg yolks with an electric mixer until fluffy and lemon-colored. Beat in the juice concentrate, 1 tablespoon (15 ml) at a time. Place the pan over very hot, not boiling, water and continue to beat the yolks while slowly and gradually adding the Marsala. Beat until smooth, fluffy and thick, about 10 minutes. Remove from heat and cool pan in a bowl of cold water.

Whip the cream until stiff but not dry; gently fold it into the cooled yolk mixture. Remove the glasses from the refrigerator, wipe any condensation off with a clean towel, and gently turn the zabaglione into the glasses, leaving a space of at least 1 inch (2.5 cm) at the top of each glass. Cover each glass tightly with foil and place in the freezer for at least 3 hours, or until firm.

Prepare Chocolate Sauce, but substitute the same Marsala used in the Zabaglione recipe for the Pedro Ximenez wine. Substitute frozen unsweetened orange juice concentrate for the apple juice concentrate. When the sauce is cool, cover and chill it in the refrigerator until serving time.

To serve, remove the glasses containing zabaglione from the freezer and uncover. Pour cold Chocolate Sauce over each one and serve immediately. Handle the glasses by the stem end so as not to mar the frosted effect.

Serves 6

Gelatin Desserts

Fluffy Applesauce Mousse

2 tablespoons (14 g) unflavored gelatin
6 ounces (175 ml) frozen unsweetened apple juice
  concentrate, thawed
3 cups (750 ml) unsweetened applesauce
¼ cup (60 ml) sweet or cream sherry
½ teaspoon (2.5 ml) ground cinnamon
1 teaspoon (5 ml) grated orange rind
1 cup (250 ml) heavy cream, whipped

In a small saucepan, sprinkle the gelatin over the juice concentrate and let stand 5 minutes to soften. Place pan over medium heat, and cook, gently stirring until gelatin dissolves. Transfer dissolved gelatin into a large mixing bowl. Stir in the applesauce, sherry, cinnamon and orange rind. Chill in the refrigerator until mixture is slightly thickened or forms a mound when dropped from a spoon.

Fold whipped cream into the slightly thickened gelatin. Turn mixture into a lightly oiled 6-cup (1.5-liter) decorative mold, and chill until set, about 6 hours. Unmold before serving.

Serves 6 to 8

Apple Jacket Gelatin

1 large lemon
6 large McIntosh apples, cored
1 tablespoon (7 g) unflavored gelatin
⅓ cup (75 ml) cold water
⅓ cup (75 ml) frozen unsweetened apple juice
    concentrate, thawed
2 egg whites, at room temperature
¼ teaspoon (1.5 ml) salt

Grate the rind from the lemon and set aside. Squeeze the juice into a cup.

Cut the stem-end from the apples ½ inch (13 mm) from the top. Use a grapefruit knife to remove the apple flesh, leaving shells ⅛ inch (3 mm) thick. Brush the inside of the shells with lemon juice. Wrap them in plastic wrap and refrigerate.

Dice the apple flesh and put it together with the remaining lemon juice in a small saucepan. Bring to a boil, lower heat, cover and cook for about 10 minutes until apple is tender.

Sprinkle gelatin over the cold water and let stand for 5 minutes to soften. Stir softened gelatin into the hot apple mixture until dissolved. Stir in the juice concentrate. Purée mixture in a blender. Chill until slightly thickened, or until mixture forms a mound when dropped from a spoon.

Add the salt to the egg whites and beat until stiff, but not dry. Fold into the slightly thickened apple mixture. Spoon mixture into the apple shells. Chill until set. Before serving, sprinkle with the grated lemon rind.

Serves 6

Fruits in Sherried Cream

2 tablespoons (15 g) unflavored gelatin
1½ cups (375 ml) cold water, divided
12 ounces (350 ml) frozen unsweetened orange juice
*   concentrate, thawed*
½ cup (125 ml) cream sherry or Montilla Cream
2 peaches
2 pears
1 banana
¼ cup (60 ml) freshly shredded unsweetened coconut
1 cup (250 ml) heavy cream, whipped
shredded coconut for garnish

In a small saucepan, sprinkle the gelatin over ¾ cup (175 ml) water and let stand for 5 minutes to soften. Place over medium heat and cook, gently stirring, until gelatin dissolves. Remove from heat.

In a mixing bowl, combine remaining water, the juice concentrate and the dissolved gelatin. Stir in the sherry, mixing well. Cover and chill, stirring occasionally, until slightly thickened.

Peel the fruits and cut into bite-size pieces. Immediately stir them into the slightly thickened gelatin. Stir in the coconut; fold in the whipped cream. Turn mixture into a lightly oiled decorative 6-cup (1.5-liter) mold, cover and chill until set, about 6 hours.

To serve, unmold cream onto a serving plate. Garnish with shredded coconut.

Serves 8

Green-Grape Mousse

2 tablespoons (14 g) unflavored gelatin
3 cups (750 ml) unsweetened white grape juice
1 pound (450 g) seedless green grapes, stems removed
1 teaspoon (5 ml) vanilla extract
1 cup (250 ml) heavy cream, whipped
grape clusters for garnish

Sprinkle the gelatin over 1 cup (250 ml) grape juice in a small saucepan, and let stand for 5 minutes to soften. Place over low heat, and cook, gently stirring, until gelatin dissolves. Cool to room temperature. Add dissolved gelatin to remaining grape juice. Pour a very thin layer into the bottom of a decorative 6-cup (1.5-liter) mold. Chill until nearly set. Arrange at least one fourth of the grapes in a pattern on top of the nearly set gelatin. Spoon over another thin layer of gelatin mixture and chill to set the design. Cover remaining gelatin mixture in a separate bowl and chill, stirring occasionally, until slightly thickened.

Remove the mold containing the design from the refrigerator. Halve the remaining grapes and stir them and the vanilla into the slightly thickened gelatin. Fold in the whipped cream. Turn this mixture into the mold on top of the set pattern. Cover and chill until completely set, about 5 hours.

Unmold to serve. Garnish with small clusters of grapes at the base of the mold.

Serves 6

Honeydew Mousse

1 honeydew melon
4 teaspoons (20 ml) unflavored gelatin
1¾ cups (425 ml) unsweetened white grape juice
2 tablespoons (30 ml) grated lime rind
¾ cup (175 ml) heavy cream, whipped

Cut the melon in half lengthways and discard the seeds. Use a teaspoon or a small melon-ball cutter to remove as much of the melon as possible without puncturing the rind. Place melon pieces in a bowl and chill. Chill the melon halves until ready for use.

In a heat-resistant cup, sprinkle the gelatin over ½ cup (125 ml) of the grape juice, and let stand 5 minutes to soften. Place cup in a pan of very hot water until gelatin dissolves. Stir dissolved gelatin into the remaining grape juice, using a rubber spatula to scrape the cup clean. Chill mixture until slightly thickened.

Stir chilled melon balls and lime rind into the slightly thickened mixture. Fold in the whipped cream. Turn mixture into the melon rind halves, cover and chill until set, about 4 hours.

To serve, cut melon halves into wedges.

Serves 4 to 6

Macédoine Mousse

1 tablespoon (7 g) unflavored gelatin
6 ounces (175 ml) frozen unsweetened juice
*   concentrate (any flavor), thawed*
1 tablespoon (15 ml) grated lemon rind
1 cup (225 g) dairy sour cream
½ pound (225 g) green seedless grapes
2 ripe pears, peeled and diced
2 ripe peaches, peeled and diced
1 ripe banana, peeled and sliced
½ cup (125 ml) heavy cream, whipped

Do not prepare the fruit until the gelatin is slightly thickened. At that point it may be peeled and cut up directly into the mixture to prevent it browning.

Sprinkle the gelatin over the juice concentrate in a small saucepan and let stand for 5 minutes to soften. Cook over medium heat, gently stirring, until the gelatin is dissolved. Remove from heat, stir in the lemon rind, and cool to room temperature. Stir in the sour cream, then chill until mixture is slightly thickened or forms a mound when dropped from a spoon.

Select 6 small clusters of grapes and set them in the refrigerator for garnish. Pluck remaining grapes off their stems and stir them into the slightly thickened gelatin. Prepare remaining fruits and stir them into the gelatin. Fold in the whipped cream. Turn mixture into a lightly oiled decorative 1-quart (1-liter) mold, cover, and chill until set, about 5 hours.

To serve, unmold gelatin onto a serving plate and garnish with the reserved grape clusters. Additional whipped cream may be used for garnish, if desired.

Serves 6

Fresh Strawberry-Rhubarb Mousse

4 teaspoons (9.5 g) unflavored gelatin
¼ cup (60 ml) cold water or sweet white table wine
Strawberry-Rhubarb Sauce (page 74)
1 cup (250 ml) heavy cream, whipped

In a small heat-resistant cup, sprinkle the gelatin over the water or wine and let stand for 5 minutes to soften. Set cup in a pan of very hot water, until gelatin dissolves. Measure 1¾ cups (450 ml) Strawberry-Rhubarb Sauce into a mixing bowl. Using a rubber spatula to clean the cup well, scrape the dissolved gelatin into the sauce and stir it in thoroughly. Chill, stirring occasionally, until slightly thickened.

Fold the whipped cream into the slightly thickened gelatin. Turn into a decorative 1-quart (1-liter) mold, cover, and chill until set, about 4 hours.

To serve, unmold mousse onto a serving plate. Serve remaining Strawberry-Rhubarb Sauce on the side or pour it over the mousse.

Serves 6

Nectarine Chiffon Pie

½ cup (125 ml) frozen unsweetened orange juice
  concentrate, thawed
3 eggs, separated
1 tablespoon (7 g) unflavored gelatin
5 nectarines, peeled and sliced
1 teaspoon (5 ml) grated orange rind
½ cup (125 ml) heavy cream
9-inch (23-cm) pie shell, baked and cooled
1 nectarine, sliced for garnish
whipped cream for garnish

Beat the juice concentrate with the egg yolks in a saucepan; sprinkle the gelatin over and let stand for 5 minutes to soften. Cook over low heat, stirring constantly, until mixture thickens slightly and just begins to bubble. Do not boil. Remove from heat.

Purée the nectarines in a blender, then stir the purée, together with the grated orange rind, into the custard. Cover with plastic wrap and chill until mixture forms a mound when dropped from a spoon.

Beat the cream with an electric mixer until it stands in peaks. Use the same beaters to beat the gelatin mixture to remove any lumps. Fold the cream into the gelatin. Clean the beaters and beat the egg whites until stiff; fold them into the gelatin mixture. Turn into the pie shell; chill until firm.

To serve, garnish with nectarine slices and whipped cream.

Serves 6 to 8

Peaches 'n Cream Mousse

4 egg yolks
1 cup (250 ml) half-and-half
½ cup (125 ml) milk
2 tablespoons (14 g) unflavored gelatin
5 large ripe peaches, peeled and sliced
1 cup (250 ml) Mirassou Fleuri Blanc or other sweet
  white table wine
1 cup (250 ml) heavy cream, whipped
peach concentrate, chilled

Beat the egg yolks, half-and-half and milk in a saucepan. Sprinkle the gelatin over and let stand for 5 minutes to soften. Place over low heat and cook, stirring constantly, until the mixture slightly thickens and just begins to bubble. Do not let boil. Remove from heat.

Purée peaches in a blender, then fold them into the custard; stir in the wine. Refrigerate, stirring occasionally, until mixture is slightly thickened and forms a soft mound when dropped from a spoon. Fold in the whipped cream. Turn into a lightly oiled decorative 6-cup (1.5-liter) mold, cover and chill until completely set, about 4 hours longer.

To serve, unmold gelatin on a serving dish and drizzle with peach concentrate.

Serves 8

Orange Rice Mousse

1 cup (200 g) uncooked long-grain rice
2½ cups (625 ml) milk, scalded
1 teaspoon (5 ml) vanilla extract
3 tablespoons (45 ml) grated orange rind
1 tablespoon (15 ml) unflavored gelatin
6 ounces (175 ml) frozen unsweetened orange juice
*   concentrate, thawed*
1 egg yolk
1 cup (250 ml) heavy cream, whipped
2 navel oranges, sectioned
Spanish Orange Sauce (page 73)

In a medium-size saucepan, combine the rice, milk, vanilla and orange rind. Bring to a boil, lower heat, cover and simmer very gently for 30 minutes, or until rice is soft and creamy.

While the rice is cooking, sprinkle the gelatin over the juice concentrate in a small mixing bowl, and let stand for 5 minutes to soften. Beat in the egg yolk. Add this mixture to the hot creamy rice, stirring over low heat until thoroughly mixed and the gelatin is dissolved. Remove from heat; cool slightly, then chill, stirring occasionally, until mixture is slightly thickened. Fold in the whipped cream. Turn mixture into a lightly oiled 6-cup (1.5-liter) mold, cover, and chill until set, about 7 hours.

To serve, unmold mousse on a serving plate. Garnish with the orange sections, and drizzle a small amount of the sauce over the top. Serve remaining sauce on the side.

Serves 8

Pineapple Mousse

1 tablespoon (7 g) unflavored gelatin
¼ cup (60 ml) sweet or cream sherry
6 ounces (175 ml) frozen unsweetened pineapple juice
    concentrate, thawed
8 ounces (250 ml) unsweetened canned crushed
    pineapple*
cold water
¾ cup (175 ml) heavy cream, whipped

Sprinkle the gelatin over the sherry in a small heat-resistant cup and let stand for 5 minutes to soften. Place cup in a pan of very hot water until gelatin dissolves.

In a large mixing bowl, add the dissolved gelatin to the pineapple juice concentrate, using a rubber spatula to scrape out the cup. Drain the crushed pineapple. Set the pineapple aside, and add enough cold water to the liquid to equal ¾ cup (175 ml). Stir this liquid into the gelatin mixture. Chill gelatin until slightly thickened or until mixture forms a mound when dropped from a spoon.

Stir crushed pineapple into the slightly thickened gelatin. Fold in the whipped cream. Turn mixture into a lightly oiled 1-quart (1-liter) decorative mold, and chill until set, about 5 hours. Unmold before serving.

Serves 6

*Do not use fresh pineapple in this recipe because it prevents the jelling process.

Ported Prune Mousse

2½ cups (625 ml) water
1 Valencia juice orange
1 cup (225 g) pitted prunes
4 teaspoons (9.5 g) unflavored gelatin
3 tablespoons (45 ml) ruby port
1 cup (250 ml) heavy cream
1 tablespoon (15 ml) apple concentrate

Bring the water to a boil in a small saucepan. Peel the orange and cut the rind into julienne strips. Blanch the strips in the boiling water for 1 minute, then refresh in cold water. Drain the strips (reserve the water) and dry them on paper toweling, then place in the refrigerator to chill.

Add the prunes to the orange peel water, return to a boil, cover, and simmer gently for 20 minutes. Set aside to cool slightly.

Squeeze the juice of the orange into a cup and sprinkle the gelatin over it; let stand for 5 minutes to soften.

Using a slotted spoon, transfer the prunes to a blender container and process until smooth. Add the softened gelatin and gradually add the prune liquid to the purée, blending until well mixed and the gelatin is dissolved. Blend in the wine. Transfer to a mixing bowl, cover, and chill until slightly thickened.

Beat the heavy cream until it begins to thicken. Add the apple concentrate and continue beating until stiff but not dry. Using the same beater, whip the prune-gelatin mixture to dissolve any lumps. Fold in half of the whipped cream. Turn the mixture into 6 individual parfait glasses or pudding cups. Chill until set, about 3 hours. Cover and refrigerate the remaining whipped cream.

To serve, garnish each serving with a dollop of the reserved whipped cream and top with the julienne orange strips.

Serves 6

No-Bake Pineapple Cheesecake

6 ounces (175 ml) frozen unsweetened pineapple juice
  concentrate, thawed
2 tablespoons (14 g) unflavored gelatin
2 eggs, separated
3 cups (750 ml) cottage cheese
8 ounces (250 ml) canned unsweetened crushed
  pineapple
1 teaspoon (5 ml) vanilla extract
½ cup (125 ml) heavy cream, whipped

Sprinkle the gelatin over the juice concentrate in a small saucepan and let stand for 5 minutes to soften. Lightly beat the egg yolks and stir into the gelatin mixture. Cook over low heat, stirring constantly, until gelatin dissolves and mixture is slightly thickened. Do not allow to boil, or it will curdle. Remove from heat and cool slightly. Process mixture in a blender with the cottage cheese until smooth. Transfer mixture to a large mixing bowl and stir in the crushed pineapple and the vanilla extract. Refrigerate until mixture forms a mound when dropped from a spoon.

Beat the egg whites until stiff, but not dry. Fold the whipped cream into the gelatin mixture. Fold in the beaten egg whites. Turn mixture into a lightly oiled 6-cup (1.5-liter) decorative mold, and chill until set, about 6 hours. Unmold before serving.

Serves 8

Red Sangría Shimmer

2 tablespoons (14 g) unflavored gelatin
¼ cup (60 ml) frozen unsweetened orange juice
  concentrate, thawed
1 tablespoon (15 ml) fresh lemon juice
2½ cups (625 ml) Lambrusco red wine*
⅔ cup (150 ml) club soda
2 peaches, peeled and diced
1 large sweet plum, cut into bite-size pieces
1 cup (250 ml) strawberries, hulled and halved

Sprinkle the gelatin over the combined juice concentrate and lemon juice in a small heat-resistant cup; let stand for 5 minutes to soften. Set cup in a pan of very hot water until gelatin is dissolved. Pour the wine into a large mixing bowl. Using a rubber spatula to scrape the cup clean, transfer the dissolved gelatin to the wine; stir to mix thoroughly. Stir in the club soda. Cover and chill, stirring occasionally, until slightly thickened.

When the gelatin is slightly thickened, prepare the fruits and immediately stir them in. Turn the mixture into a decorative 6-cup (1.5-liter) mold that has been rinsed in cold water. Cover and chill until completely set, about 6 hours or longer.

Unmold to serve.

Serves 6

*To make White Sangría, substitute a medium-sweet white wine.

Roquefort Mousse

6 egg yolks
6 tablespoons (90 ml) half-and-half
4 teaspoons (9.5 g) unflavored gelatin
¼ cup (60 ml) cold water or sweet white table wine
¾ pound (350 g) Roquefort cheese*
¾ cup (175 ml) heavy cream, whipped
3 egg whites
6 perfect walnut halves, unsalted (for garnish)
6 ripe persimmons, chilled, or assorted fruits in season

In the top part of a double boiler, beat the egg yolks with an electric mixer until light and fluffy; beat in the half-and-half. Sprinkle the gelatin over the water in a small cup and let stand for 5 minutes to soften. Add softened gelatin to the yolk mixture. Place over very hot water and cook, stirring constantly, until the mixture thickens and gelatin dissolves. Do not let water boil. Force the cheese through a sieve, and add it to the yolk mixture. Continue stirring until thoroughly combined. Remove from heat and cool to room temperature, stirring occasionally.

Fold the whipped cream into the gelatin mixture. Beat the egg whites until stiff, and fold them in. Turn into a decorative 3-cup (750 ml) mold, cover, and chill until set, about 4 hours.

To serve, unmold mousse on a serving plate and garnish with the walnut halves. Surround with persimmons or other fruit. A chilled glass of Sauternes or Asti Spumante is a delightful accompaniment to this dessert. Or consider serving it with a fine Porto.

Serves 6

*Stilton or Gorgonzola may be substituted.

Roquefort Mousse
with Sauternes Peaches

1 tablespoon (7 g) unflavored gelatin
2 cups (500 ml) French Sauternes*, divided into 2
   equal parts
8 ounces (225 g) Roquefort cheese
¾ cup (175 ml) heavy cream
8 large ripe freestone peaches

Sprinkle the gelatin over 1 cup (250 ml) Sauternes in a small saucepan and let stand for 5 minutes to soften. Place over low heat to dissolve gelatin, stirring occasionally. Gradually beat the dissolved gelatin into the cheese. Whip the cream until it stands in peaks; fold it into the cheese mixture. Lightly oil a decorative 1-quart (1-liter) mold and turn the cheese mixture into it. Chill until set, about 5 hours.

Dip each peach into boiling water for 20 to 30 seconds, and then immediately plunge it into ice water. The skins will now easily peel off. Halve and pit the peeled peaches, then cut them into ¼-inch (6-mm) slices. Macerate them in the remaining 1 cup (250 ml) Sauternes in a serving bowl. Cover and chill until serving time.

To serve, unmold the gelatin on a serving dish and place the chilled Sauternes peaches alongside.

Serves 8

---

*Sauternes is the classic wine to serve with Roquefort. However, you may substitute any other sweet, golden table wine, if desired. Other fruits may also be substituted for the peaches.

Sauternes Sabayon Mousse

6 egg yolks
2 tablespoons (14 g) unflavored gelatin
2 cups (500 ml) French Sauternes*, divided
2 cups (500 ml) heavy cream, whipped
small clusters of seedless green grapes
fresh mint leaves (optional)

In a small saucepan, beat the egg yolks with an electric mixer or whisk until light and lemon-colored. Sprinkle the gelatin over ½ cup (125 ml) of the wine and let stand for 5 minutes to soften. Gradually beat remaining wine into the beaten egg yolks. When the gelatin is soft, add it to the yolk mixture. Place the pan over medium-low heat and cook, stirring constantly, until the mixture thickens; do not allow it to boil. Remove from heat, immediately cover with plastic wrap, and cool to room temperature. When completely cool, fold in the whipped cream.

Turn mousse mixture into a lightly oiled 6-cup (1.5-liter) mold or 8 large unoiled balloon wineglasses. Cover and chill until set, about 6 hours for the large mold or 2 hours for the individual servings.

To serve, turn out the large mold on a serving plate. If using wineglasses, do not unmold. Garnish with grape clusters and mint leaves. Serve cold.

Serves 8

*Other sweet white table wines may be substituted for the Sauternes.

Spanish Cream

1 tablespoon (7 g) unflavored gelatin
¼ cup (60 ml) sweet or cream sherry
½ cup (125 ml) light cream or half-and-half
½ cup (125 ml) frozen unsweetened orange juice
*   concentrate, thawed*
⅔ cup (150 ml) heavy cream, whipped
1 cup (250 ml) fresh strawberries or raspberries

Sprinkle the gelatin over the sherry in a heat-resistant cup and let stand for 5 minutes to soften. Set the cup in a pan of very hot water; stir gently until gelatin is dissolved.

Combine the light cream and juice concentrate in a small mixing bowl. Add the dissolved gelatin, scraping it out of the cup with a rubber spatula; whisk or beat until thoroughly mixed. Cover and chill, stirring occasionally, until slightly thickened. When the mixture has the consistency of unbeaten egg white, fold in the whipped cream.

Divide mixture among 4 individual sherbet glasses or balloon wineglasses, cover, and chill until set. Just before serving, garnish with strawberries or raspberries. Serve cold.

Serves 4

Note: To make a larger mold, turn mixture into a lightly oiled decorative 3-cup (750 ml) mold; chill until set; unmold before serving. Garnish with the berries.

Watermelon Strawberry Delight

4 pounds (1.8 kg) watermelon, weighed with rind
2 cups (500 ml) fresh strawberries, hulled
2 tablespoons (14 g) unflavored gelatin

Scoop out the melon and remove the seeds. Purée half of the strawberries with all the melon in a blender. Measure the purée; you will need 3¾ cups (925 ml). From this amount, measure out ½ cup (125 ml) purée. Place the small amount in a heat-resistant cup and sprinkle the gelatin over the top. Let stand for 5 minutes to soften. Set cup in a pan of very hot water and stir gently until the gelatin is dissolved. Stir the dissolved gelatin into the remaining 3¼ cups (800 ml) purée. Cover and chill, stirring occasionally, until slightly thickened.

Slice the remaining strawberries. Stir them into the slightly thickened gelatin. Rinse a decorative 5-cup (1.2-liter) mold in cold water; pour the gelatin mixture into it. Cover and chill until set, about 5 hours or longer.

Unmold to serve.

Serves 6

Puddings, Custards and Dessert Omelets

Apple Sour-Cream Dessert Omelet

2 tablespoons (30 g) butter
4 large Cortland or York apples
¼ cup (60 ml) frozen unsweetened apple juice
    concentrate
1 tablespoon (15 ml) Pedro Ximenez or other sweet
    fortified wine
4 eggs, separated
½ cup (125 g) dairy sour cream
16 ounces (450 g) unsweetened applesauce
cinnamon
additional sour cream for garnish

Preheat oven to 350°F. (180°C.). Melt the butter in an 8-inch (20-cm) ovenproof omelet pan or skillet. Peel and core apples. Cut them into ¼-inch (6-mm) slices, and sauté the slices in the butter for 1 minute on each side. Add the apple juice concentrate and the wine; cook for an additional 5 minutes.

Beat the egg yolks until thick; beat in the sour cream. Beat the egg whites until stiff but not dry. Fold the yolk mixture into the whites, and pour over the apple slices. Bake for about 20 minutes, until omelet is puffy and golden. Warm the applesauce in a pan on top of the stove while the omelet is baking. Serve the omelet hot with the warm applesauce, cinnamon and additional sour cream.

Serves 4 to 6

Peach Omelet

6 eggs
2 tablespoons (30 ml) heavy cream or half-and-half
3 tablespoons (45 ml) frozen unsweetened orange
   juice concentrate, thawed
4 tablespoons (60 g) butter
3 large ripe peaches, peeled and sliced
⅔ cup (150 g) dairy sour cream
peach concentrate

Beat eggs, cream and juice concentrate lightly in a mixing bowl. Melt butter in a 10-inch (25-cm) omelet pan or skillet, tipping pan to coat bottom and sides. Pour egg mixture into pan and cook over medium heat, lifting edges of set mixture to allow uncooked egg to flow beneath. Continue to cook for about 1 minute, until omelet is set but top is still moist. Layer peach slices over the top of the omelet; spoon the sour cream over the peaches; cook for 30 seconds. Fold omelet into thirds, then slide onto a serving plate. Drizzle peach concentrate over the top.

Serves 4

Baked Apple Charlotte

10 large Delicious apples, peeled
6 tablespoons (90 g) butter, divided
3 tablespoons (45 ml) apple concentrate
1 tablespoon (15 ml) grated orange or lemon rind
1 teaspoon (5 ml) vanilla extract
3 tablespoons (45 ml) Apricot-Pineapple Preserves
  (page 75)
3 tablespoons (45 ml) Pedro Ximenez or other sweet
  fortified wine
15 thin slices of dry (not hard) whole-wheat bread
1 egg yolk, lightly beaten
Spanish Orange Sauce (page 73)

Core apples and cut fruit into 1/8-inch (3-mm) slices. Melt 4 table-spoons (60 g) butter in a large frying pan. Add the apple slices and sauté until they start to brown. Add concentrate, grated rind and vanilla, stirring until mixed. Cover and cook over low heat, stirring occasionally, for about 20 minutes, or until all liquid is evaporated. Stir in preserves and wine and continue cooking, uncovered, until mixture is very thick, about 10 minutes. Cool slightly.

Preheat oven to 450°F. (220°C.). Grease a 6-cup (1.5-liter) soufflé dish or charlotte mold with the remaining 2 tablespoons (30 g) butter. Trim crusts from bread. Cut 3 slices of bread into 4 triangles each; arrange the 12 triangles slightly overlapping around the bottom of the dish. Use a 2-inch (5-cm) cookie cutter to cut off the tips of the arranged triangles, leaving a circle in the center of the dish. Cut a circle with the cookie cutter from another slice of bread and place it in the hole. Slice the remaining bread into lengthwise halves, and arrange 14 of the halves in overlapping slices around the sides of the dish. The slices may extend slightly higher than the rim of the dish.

Stir the egg yolk into the slightly cooled apple purée. Turn the mixture into the bread-lined dish. Use remaining bread halves to cover the purée, trimming to fit as neatly as possible. Cover the top with a circle of wax paper. Bake for 40 to 45 minutes. Remove from oven, remove wax paper, and allow to cool on a wire rack for 1½ hours. The charlotte will settle as it cools. Using scissors, carefully trim off any extended edges of bread to the level of the pudding.

To serve, gently invert the pudding on a serving plate. Pour Spanish Orange Sauce over the dessert and serve while still warm. Leftovers may be served cold.

Serves 6 to 8

Baked Orange Custard

1 ½ cups (375 ml) half-and-half or light cream
3 whole eggs, lightly beaten
1 extra egg yolk, lightly beaten
1 cup (250 ml) frozen unsweetened orange juice
  concentrate, thawed
1 navel orange, for garnish

Preheat oven to 325°F. (165°C.). Combine the first 4 ingredients in a mixing bowl and blend well. Finely grate 2 teaspoons (10 ml) of the orange rind and add it to the mixture.

Pour into individual custard cups and set them in a baking pan of hot water. Bake for 40 to 50 minutes, or until a knife inserted in the center comes out clean. Cool, then chill in the refrigerator.

To serve, peel and section the orange. Place an orange section on top of each custard for garnish. Serve cold.

Serves 6

Baked Sherry Custards

4 eggs, lightly beaten
1 cup (250 ml) heavy cream, divided
1¾ cups (450 ml) milk, scalded
½ cup (125 ml) sweet or cream sherry
1 teaspoon (5 ml) vanilla extract
1 tablespoon (15 ml) sweet or cream sherry
2 tablespoons (15 g) chopped almonds

Preheat oven to 325°F. (165°C.). In a medium-size mixing bowl, beat the eggs with ½ cup (125 ml) heavy cream. Continue beating while gradually adding the hot milk. Beat in the ½ cup (125 ml) sherry and the vanilla.

Butter 6 individual custard cups. Divide the mixture among the cups. Set cups in a shallow baking pan and pour in about 1 inch (2.5 cm) of very hot water to surround cups. Bake for 45 minutes, or until custards are set in the center. Remove cups from hot water and cool. Chill in the refrigerator. Serve cold.

To serve, beat remaining ½ cup (125 ml) heavy cream until it stands in peaks. Beat in the 1 tablespoon (15 ml) sherry. Top each custard cup with a dollop of whipped cream. Sprinkle each with 1 teaspoon (2.5 g) chopped almonds.

Serves 6

Apple Bread Pudding

2 cups (500 ml) stale bread cubes
1 ¾ cups (450 ml) milk, scalded
1 ¼ cups (300 ml) frozen unsweetened apple juice
　concentrate, thawed
2 eggs, beaten
¼ teaspoon (1.5 ml) ground cinnamon
¼ teaspoon (1.5 ml) ground mace
¼ teaspoon (1.5 ml) ground nutmeg
½ cup (85 g) golden raisins
butter
whipped cream

Preheat oven to 375°F. (190°C.). Place the bread cubes and hot milk in a large mixing bowl and let stand for 10 minutes. Add the juice concentrate, eggs, spices and raisins, mixing well.

Generously butter 6 individual molds or custard cups. Divide the bread mixture among the molds and dot with additional butter. Set molds in a pan of hot water and bake for 30 to 40 minutes, or until a knife inserted 1 inch (2.5 cm) from the edge comes out clean. Cool, then chill in the refrigerator.

Unmold and serve with whipped cream. The cream does not have to be sweetened since the puddings are sweet enough.

Serves 6

Poached Apricot Dumplings

Poaching liquid:
2½ cups (575 ml) water
1-inch (2.5-cm) piece of ginger root, peeled
6 ounces (175 ml) frozen unsweetened orange juice
　　concentrate, thawed

Batter:
1¼ cups (150 g) flour
2 teaspoons (10 ml) baking soda
½ teaspoon (2.5 ml) ground cinnamon
1 tablespoon (15 g) butter
¼ pound (100 g) sun-dried apricots, chopped
½ cup (125 ml) milk

For the poaching liquid, combine the water, ginger root, and all but 1 tablespoon (15 ml) of the juice concentrate in a wide saucepan with a tight-fitting lid. Bring the liquid to a boil, lower the heat, cover, and simmer gently while preparing the batter.

Sift the flour, baking soda and cinnamon into a large mixing bowl. Add the butter and rub it into the dry ingredients with your fingers. Stir in the fruit, milk and the reserved tablespoon (15 ml) of the juice concentrate to make a batter.

Working very quickly, drop spoonfuls of the batter into the simmering poaching liquid. Cover the pan and simmer very gently for 25 minutes. Do not lift the lid during this time. Remove from heat and cool slightly.

Serve the dumplings warm in individual serving dishes with some of the poaching liquid spooned over. Discard the piece of ginger root.

Serves 6

Steamed Date or Fig Pudding

2 tablespoons (30 g) butter
6 ounces (175 ml) frozen unsweetened apple juice
concentrate, thawed
1 egg
8 ounces (225 g) pressed dates or figs, chopped
1¼ cups (150 g) flour
¼ teaspoon (1.5 ml) salt
½ teaspoon (2.5 ml) baking powder
¼ teaspoon (1.5 ml) baking soda
Sherry Sauce (page 73)

Melt the butter in a large saucepan; remove from heat. Stir in the juice concentrate and the egg and beat until thoroughly mixed. Stir in the fruit. Sift the dry ingredients and stir them into the liquid to make a smooth batter.

Grease a 1-quart (1-liter) pudding mold or bowl or individual pudding molds. Fill two thirds full with the batter. Cover tightly. Steam the large mold for 2 hours or the small molds for 1 hour. Turn out and serve warm with Sherry Sauce.

Serves 4 or 5

Surprise Apple Soufflés

2 cups (500 ml) thick unsweetened applesauce
2 tablespoons (30 ml) frozen unsweetened orange or
  apple juice concentrate, thawed
½ teaspoon (2.5 ml) ground cinnamon, divided
24 raisins
4 egg whites

Combine the applesauce, juice concentrate and ¼ teaspoon (1.5 ml) cinnamon in a mixing bowl, stirring well. Spoon 1 tablespoon (15 ml) applesauce mixture into each of six 6-ounce (175 ml) ovenproof custard cups. Place 4 raisins on each spoonful of applesauce.

Shortly before serving, preheat oven to 350°F. (180°C.). Beat the egg whites until they stand in peaks. Gently fold the whites into the remaining applesauce. Spoon the mixture into the custard cups and sprinkle with the remaining cinnamon. Pour about 1 inch (2.5 cm) of hot water into a baking dish and set the cups in the water. Bake for 15 to 20 minutes, or until puffed and golden. Serve immediately.

Serves 6

Coconut Soufflé

3 tablespoons (45 g) butter
3 tablespoons (45 ml) flour
⅔ cup (150 ml) half-and-half or milk
6 tablespoons (90 ml) frozen unsweetened juice
   concentrate (any flavor), thawed
4 egg yolks
1 teaspoon (5 ml) vanilla extract
1½ cups (375 ml) grated fresh coconut
5 egg whites
2 tablespoons (30 ml) shredded fresh coconut

Melt the butter in a saucepan; add the flour and cook until bubbly. Remove from heat; gradually stir in the half-and-half. Return to heat and cook, stirring constantly, until thickened. Remove from heat. Beat the juice concentrate and egg yolks together; beat into the thickened sauce. Transfer to a large mixing bowl. Stir in the vanilla and the grated coconut.

About 50 minutes before serving, preheat oven to 375°F. (190°C.). Butter a 6-cup or 2-quart (1.5- or 2-liter) soufflé dish. Beat the egg whites until stiff but not dry. Fold half of the beaten whites into the coconut mixture; gently fold remaining egg whites into the mixture. Turn into the soufflé dish; sprinkle with the shredded coconut. Bake for 40 to 45 minutes, until puffed and golden. Serve immediately.

Serves 6

Peach Soufflé with Marsala

2 cups (500 ml) diced, peeled fresh peaches
3 tablespoons (45 ml) frozen unsweetened orange
  juice concentrate, thawed
¼ cup (60 ml) chopped almonds
3 tablespoons (45 g) butter
3 tablespoons (45 ml) flour
⅔ cup (150 ml) milk
4 egg yolks
⅓ cup (75 ml) sweet Marsala or Florio Almond Cream
  Marsala
5 egg whites

Preheat oven to 375°F. (190°C.). Butter a 2-quart (2-liter) soufflé dish. Mix the peaches with the juice concentrate and place the mixture in the bottom of the soufflé dish; sprinkle with the almonds; set aside.

Melt the butter in a saucepan, add the flour, and cook until bubbly. Remove from heat; gradually stir in the milk. Return to heat and cook, stirring constantly, until thickened. Remove from heat. Beat the egg yolks with the Marsala; beat into the thickened sauce. Transfer to a large mixing bowl.

Beat the egg whites until stiff but not dry. Fold half into the thickened sauce; gently fold remaining egg whites into the sauce. Pour over the peaches and almonds in the soufflé dish. Bake for 40 to 45 minutes, until puffed and golden. Serve immediately.

Serves 6

Pumpkin Soufflé

A traditional flavor, yet a different dessert for Thanksgiving or Halloween

1½ pounds (.67 kg) fresh pumpkin (a small one)
5 eggs, separated
6 ounces (175 ml) frozen unsweetened orange juice
  concentrate, thawed
3 tablespoons (45 ml) cream sherry or sweet sherry
½ teaspoon (2.5 ml) ground ginger
½ teaspoon (2.5 ml) ground cloves
½ teaspoon (2.5 ml) ground nutmeg
¾ teaspoon (4 ml) ground cinnamon
½ teaspoon (2.5 ml) salt
Coconut Cream Topping (page 70)

Peel the pumpkin, remove the seeds, and cut into small cubes. Cook in boiling water until tender, about 30 minutes. Drain and mash. Cool slightly.

Preheat oven to 350°F. (180°C.). Beat the egg yolks until thick and lemon-colored, about 7 minutes. In a large mixing bowl, combine the pumpkin, egg yolks, juice concentrate, sherry, spices and salt, mixing well. Beat the egg whites until stiff but not dry. Fold half of the whites into the pumpkin mixture; gently fold in remaining whites.

Turn mixture into a buttered 6-cup (1.5-liter) soufflé dish. Bake for 40 to 45 minutes, until puffed and golden. Serve immediately with Coconut Cream Topping.

Serves 6

Coeur à la Crème

16 ounces (450 g) cottage cheese
8 ounces (225 g) cream cheese, at room temperature
pinch of salt
1 ½ cups (375 ml) heavy cream
1 ½ teaspoons (7.5 ml) grape concentrate
1 pint (225 g) fresh strawberries, hulled and halved
2 tablespoons (30 ml) grape concentrate

Beat the cottage cheese and cream cheese in a large mixing bowl until combined. Add the salt and continue beating with an electric mixer while gradually adding the cream; beat until smooth and thick. Beat in the 1 ½ teaspoons (7.5 ml) grape concentrate.

Transfer the mixture to a large *coeur à la crème* mold. Alternatively, line a bowl-shaped strainer or a woven bowl-shaped basket with muslin and press in the cheese mixture. (The container must have holes so that the liquid can drain out.) Place the mold, strainer or basket into a deep dish, which will catch the drips. Cover with plastic wrap and refrigerate overnight.

Prepare the berries shortly before serving and toss them with the remaining grape concentrate to sweeten. Unmold the *crème* onto a serving dish or platter and surround with the berries. Serve immediately.

Serves 6 to 8

Ported Dessert Cheese

16 ounces (450 g) cream cheese, at room temperature
4 tablespoons (60 g) butter, at room temperature
3 tablespoons (45 ml) ruby port
1 tablespoon (15 ml) grated orange rind
½ teaspoon (2.5 ml) ground coriander
¼ teaspoon (1.5 ml) ground cinnamon
⅛ teaspoon (.5 ml) ground ginger
½ cup (60 g) finely chopped almonds

In a medium-size mixing bowl, combine the cheese, butter, port, orange rind and spices; beat well with a wooden spoon until blended. Chill until easy to handle. Shape mixture into a ball and roll in the chopped almonds. Place the ball on a dish, carefully cover with plastic wrap, and chill overnight.

Serve with crisp crackers, fruit and the port remaining in the bottle.

Serves 6 to 8

Ported Plum Streusel

Filling:

6 cups (1.5. liter) Italian fresh prune plums, halved and pitted

1 teaspoon (5 ml) cinnamon

¼ cup (60 ml) frozen unsweetened orange juice concentrate, thawed

2 tablespoons (30 ml) water

¼ cup (60 ml) ruby port

1 tablespoon (15 ml) grated orange rind

1 tablespoon (15 ml) quick-cooking tapioca

Follow directions for Apple-Raisin Streusel (page 65). Almonds may be substituted for the pecans when making the topping, if desired. Orange juice concentrate should replace the apple juice concentrate in the topping recipe.

Serves 6

Cheddar Apple Dowdy

4 slices of day-old bread
2 tablespoons (30 ml) butter, softened
5 cups (1.2 l) sliced McIntosh or York apples
½ cup (125 ml) golden raisins
½ teaspoon (2.5 ml) cinnamon
½ teaspoon (2.5 ml) nutmeg
¼ cup (60 ml) frozen unsweetened apple cider
* concentrate, thawed*
¼ cup (60 ml) water
2 tablespoons (30 ml) sweet sherry or cream sherry
¼ cup (60 ml) butter, divided in half
1 cup (250 ml) Cheddar cheese, grated

Preheat oven to 350°F. (180°C.). Butter a 6-cup (1.5-liter) baking dish.

Butter each slice of bread and arrange in baking dish, buttered-side up. In a large mixing bowl, combine the apples, raisins, cinnamon, nutmeg, juice concentrate, water and sherry. Toss to mix. Place mixture on top of bread slices. Dot with 2 tablespoons (30 ml) of the butter. Cover and bake for 30 minutes.

Remove cover. Sprinkle with the grated cheese. Dot with remaining butter. Bake uncovered for an additional 20 minutes. Serve warm.

Serves 6

Pineapple-Tapioca Dessert

2½ cups (625 ml) unsweetened pineapple juice
5 tablespoons (75 ml) quick-cooking tapioca
pinch salt
⅛ teaspoon (.5 ml) ground ginger
8 ounces (250 ml) unsweetened canned crushed
pineapple
2 tablespoons (30 ml) sweet or cream sherry

In a large saucepan, combine pineapple juice, tapioca, salt and ginger. Let stand for 5 minutes. Stir in the crushed pineapple. Over medium heat, heat tapioca mixture to boiling, stirring frequently. Remove from heat; let stand for 20 minutes; then stir in the sherry. Spoon mixture into 6 custard cups. Serve warm or refrigerate and serve chilled.

Serves 6

Sherried Pineapple Soufflé

2 cups (500 ml) unsweetened crushed pineapple
¼ cup (60 ml) chopped walnuts
3 tablespoons (45 g) butter
3 tablespoons (45 ml) flour
⅓ cup (80 ml) frozen unsweetened pineapple juice
  concentrate, thawed
⅓ cup (80 ml) heavy cream or half-and-half
⅓ cup (80 ml) sweet or cream sherry
4 egg yolks
5 egg whites

Preheat oven to 375°F. (190°C.) Butter a 2-quart (2-liter) soufflé dish. Spread the crushed pineapple in the bottom of the dish and sprinkle with the nuts; set aside.

Melt the butter in a saucepan, add the flour, and cook until bubbly. Remove from heat; gradually stir in the juice concentrate and the heavy cream. Return to heat and cook constantly stirring until mixture thickens. Remove from heat. Beat the sherry and egg yolks together; stir them into the thickened mixture. Transfer to a large mixing bowel.

Beat the egg whites until stiff, but not dry. Fold half into the thickened sauce; gently fold remaining whites into the sauce. Pour over the pineapple and nuts in the soufflé dish. Bake for 40 to 45 minutes, until puffed and golden. Serve immediately.

Serves 6

Apple-Raisin Streusel

Filling:

5 cups (1.2 l) sliced McIntosh or York apples
½ cup (125 ml) golden raisins
1 teaspoon (5 ml) cinnamon
½ teaspoon (2.5 ml) nutmeg
¼ cup (60 ml) frozen unsweetened apple juice
    concentrate, thawed
¼ cup (60 ml) water
1 tablespoon (15 ml) quick-cooking tapioca

Topping:

½ cup (125 ml) butter, softened
3 tablespoons (45 ml) frozen unsweetened apple juice
    concentrate, thawed
1 teaspoon (5 ml) cinnamon
¾ cup (175 ml) dried bread crumbs
½ cup (125 ml) flour
¾ cup (175 ml) chopped pecans or walnuts

Preheat oven to 400°F. (200°C.). Butter a 9-inch (23-cm) square baking dish.

Stir the filling ingredients in a mixing bowl until combined, and let stand for 15 minutes. Turn filling into the buttered baking dish.

Beat butter, concentrate and cinnamon until mixed. Work in the bread crumbs and flour. Stir in the nuts. Sprinkle this mixture over the apple filling. Bake for 30 minutes until apples are tender and topping is browned.

Serve warm or cold, with cream if desired.

Serves 6

Grated Carrot Pudding

6 ounces (175 ml) frozen unsweetened orange juice
  concentrate, thawed
4 eggs, lightly beaten
1½ cups (375 ml) milk, scalded
2 tablespoons (30 ml) sweet or cream sherry
4 tablespoons (60 ml) butter, melted
½ teaspoon (2.5 ml) ground cinnamon
¼ teaspoon (1.5 ml) allspice
¼ teaspoon (1.5 ml) salt
3 cups (750 ml) grated carrot
½ cup (125 ml) golden raisins

Preheat oven to 350°F. (180°C.). In a large mixing bowl, combine the juice concentrate, eggs, milk, sherry, butter, cinnamon, allspice and salt.

Butter a 6-cup (1.5-liter) baking dish. Sprinkle the grated carrot and raisins evenly over the bottom of the dish. Pour the egg mixture over the carrots and raisins. Place baking dish in a pan partially filled with hot water. Bake for 45 to 50 minutes, or until a knife inserted in the center comes out clean. Chill before serving.

Serves 6 to 8

Piña Colada Custards

1 cup (250 ml) half-and-half or light cream
4 eggs, lightly beaten
½ cup (125 ml) frozen unsweetened pineapple juice
  concentrate, thawed
8 ounces (250 ml) canned crushed unsweetened
  pineapple
1 teaspoon (5 ml) vanilla extract
1 cup (250 ml) grated fresh coconut

Preheat oven to 350°F. (180°C.). In a mixing bowl, beat together the half-and-half, eggs and juice concentrate. Stir in the crushed pineapple and the vanilla extract.

Lightly butter 6 custard cups and divide the grated coconut between them. Spoon the pineapple mixture over the coconut.

Place the cups in a baking pan and pour in enough hot water to surround the cups to a depth of about 2 inches (5 cm). Bake in the preheated oven for about 45 to 50 minutes, or until a knife inserted in the center comes out clean. Remove cups from water and cool. Refrigerate until serving time. Serve chilled.

Serves 6

Sweet Sauces, Toppings and Spreads

Chocolate Sauce

4 teaspoons (20 ml) unsweetened cocoa powder
1 tablespoon (15 ml) cornstarch
3 tablespoons (45 ml) Pedro Ximenez or other sweet,
  brown fortified wine
6 ounces (175 ml) frozen unsweetened apple juice
  concentrate, thawed
1 teaspoon (5 g) butter

In a small saucepan, combine the cocoa and cornstarch; add the wine, mixing until smooth. Pour the thawed juice concentrate into the cocoa mixture, stirring until mixed. Cook over low heat, stirring constantly, until mixture thickens and begins to bubble. Remove from heat and stir in the butter. Cool, cover, and chill until serving time. The mixture will thicken as it cools.

Yield: approximately ¾ cup (175 ml)

Coconut Cream Topping

½ cup (125 ml) finely grated fresh coconut
1 cup (250 ml) heavy cream, whipped

Fold the coconut into the whipped cream. Use as a topping over fresh fruits, with pies and cakes, or with any recipe calling for whipped cream topping. Prepare as close to serving time as possible.

Yield: approximately 2½ cups (625 ml)

Wine Glaze

1 teaspoon (2.5 g) unflavored gelatin
1 cup (250 ml) sweet white table wine,* chilled

In a heat-resistant 1-cup (250 ml) measuring cup, sprinkle the gelatin over ¼ cup (60 ml) of the wine. Let stand for 5 minutes to soften. Set cup in a pan of very hot water, and gently stir until the gelatin is dissolved. Remove cup from heat and pour in the remaining wine; stir to mix thoroughly. Set cup in a small bowl of ice water, and stir gelatin mixture gently until it becomes syrupy. Pour or spoon over pie as directed in recipe. If desired, add ½ drop of food coloring.

Yield: 1 cup (250 ml)

*Sauternes, Barsac, sweet Sauterne, Mirassou Fleuri Blanc, Malvasia Bianca, Muscat Canelli, etc., are among the wines suitable for this recipe.

Golden Apple Glaze

1 tablespoon (15 ml) cornstarch
2 tablespoons (30 ml) water
6 ounces (175 ml) frozen unsweetened apple juice
*   concentrate, thawed*
1 teaspoon (5 ml) vanilla extract

Place the cornstarch in a small saucepan and dissolve it with the water, stirring until smooth. Stir in the juice concentrate. Bring to a boil over medium heat, stirring constantly, and cook for about 1 minute, until clear and thick. Remove from heat, cool slightly, and stir in the vanilla. Cool to room temperature, stirring occasionally, before spooning over pie.

Yield: 1 cup (250 ml)

Fin de Nuit Cream

This cream topping is stabilized, which means that it will hold its shape for up to 2 days after being chilled. It is useful when you don't want to go to the trouble of whipping cream at the last moment or just before serving. It should immediately be placed on any chilled dessert, then the cream-decorated dessert should be returned to the refrigerator to allow the cream to set. The unchilled cream is also excellent for piping through a decorating bag.

> 1 teaspoon (2.5 g) unflavored gelatin
> 2 tablespoons (30 ml) Cresta Blanca Fin de Nuit*
> 1 cup (250 ml) heavy cream

Sprinkle the gelatin over the wine in a small heat-resistant cup; allow to stand for 5 minutes to soften. Set the cup in a pan of very hot water; allow to stand until gelatin is dissolved. Remove from hot water.

Beat the cream in a chilled bowl with chilled beaters until it is of medium-thick consistency (before it peaks). Use a rubber spatula to scrape the gelatin mixture into the cream, and continue beating until cream stands in stiff peaks. Do not overbeat; the gelatin will help the cream to keep its shape. Immediately pile the cream on a chilled dessert, or pipe it through a decorating bag. (Do not chill the whipped cream before using.) Once the cream is in place, place the decorated dessert in the refrigerator to set.

Yield: 2 cups (500 ml)

*Other sweet fortified wines may be substituted.

Sherry Sauce

3 eggs, separated
½ cup (125 ml) sweet or cream sherry
¼ cup (60 ml) light cream or half-and-half

Place the egg yolks in the top part of a double boiler and beat in the sherry and cream. Stir constantly over hot, not boiling, water until thickened. Keep warm, but not hot, until serving time.

Shortly before serving, beat the egg whites until stiff. Fold into the egg-yolk mixture thoroughly. Turn mixture into a decorative sauceboat and serve at room temperature.

Yield: approximately 1 cup (250 ml)

Spanish Orange Sauce

6 ounces (175 ml) frozen unsweetened orange juice
concentrate, thawed
1 egg
2 tablespoons (30 ml) Pedro Ximenez wine or sweet or
cream sherry

Beat all ingredients together in a small saucepan. Cook over low heat, stirring constantly, until the mixture is slightly thickened and it just begins to bubble; do not boil. Remove from heat and cool slightly. Sauce will get thicker upon standing.

Yield: approximately 1 cup (250 ml)

Strawberry-Rhubarb Sauce

This sauce may be served with ice cream, rice pudding, bread pudding, crêpes, vanilla custard or dessert omelets.

2½ cups (625 ml) sliced fresh rhubarb
6 ounces (175 ml) frozen unsweetened apple juice
    concentrate, thawed
½ cup (125 ml) water
2 tablespoons (30 ml) grated orange rind
¼ cup (60 ml) fresh orange juice
¼ teaspoon (1.5 ml) ground cinnamon
1 cup (250 ml) fresh sliced strawberry halves

In a medium-size saucepan, bring rhubarb, juice concentrate, water and orange rind to a boil; reduce heat, and simmer uncovered until rhubarb is very soft, 10 to 15 minutes. Remove from heat and let stand for 10 minutes. Stir in the orange juice, cinnamon and strawberries. Serve warm or cold.

Yield: about 3 cups (750 ml)

Apricot-Pineapple Preserves

8 ounces (225 g) dried apricots
20 ounces (567 g) canned unsweetened crushed
* pineapple*
water
2 tablespoons (30 ml) apple concentrate

Place apricots in a medium-size saucepan. Drain the pineapple juice into a measuring cup; add water so that the liquid measures 1¾ cups (450 ml). Pour liquid over the apricots and bring to a boil. Lower heat, cover with a tight-fitting lid, and simmer gently for 20 minutes, or until tender.

In a blender, purée apricots and cooking liquid with the apple concentrate until smooth. Return purée to the saucepan and stir in the crushed pineapple. Cook gently over low heat, stirring occasionally, for 5 minutes, or until the purée is heated through.

Fill jam jars and cover with lids or wax paper secured with rubber bands. Cool and store in the refrigerator.

Yield: approximately 3 cups (750 ml)

Strawberry Butter Spread

This will keep for several days in the refrigerator, or longer if frozen. It's an excellent replacement for jam, and is delicious when spread on hot rolls, muffins or toast.

1 cup (250 ml) butter, at room temperature
3 tablespoons (45 ml) frozen unsweetened orange
*   juice concentrate, thawed*
1 cup (250 ml) fresh strawberries, hulled
*   and crushed*

Beat the butter with the juice concentrate until fluffy. Beat in the crushed strawberries. Transfer mixture to a decorative bowl or earthenware crock. Refrigerate until serving.

Yield: 2 cups (500 ml)

Variation: Orange-Pineapple Butter

1 cup (250 ml) butter, at room temperature
3 tablespoons (45 ml) frozen unsweetened
*   orange juice concentrate, thawed*
8 ounces (250 ml) unsweetened crushed
*   pineapple, drained*
1 tablespoon (15 ml) grated orange rind

Beat together until blended.

Yield: 2 cups (500 ml)

Variation: Orange Butter

1 cup (250 ml) butter, at room temperature
4 tablespoons (60 ml) frozen unsweetened
*   orange juice concentrate, thawed*
2 tablespoons (30 ml) grated orange rind

Beat together until blended.

Yield: 1 cup (250 ml)

Crêpes and Pastries

Citrus Crêpes

½ cup (60 g) flour, sifted
1 teaspoon (5 ml) powdered lemon or orange peel
½ teaspoon (2.5 ml) salt
1 cup (250 ml) milk
4 eggs
3 tablespoons (45 g) butter, melted

Combine flour, powdered peel and salt in a 1-quart (1-liter) glass measuring vessel. Add half of the milk and all the eggs. Beat with a rotary beater until smooth. Add remaining milk and the melted butter, and beat until thoroughly blended. Cover and let stand in the refrigerator for 1 hour.

Heat a seasoned crêpe pan over medium heat for 2 to 3 minutes. Stir the crêpe batter, and pour just enough of the batter into the hot pan to cover the bottom. Cook for 15 to 30 seconds, or until the surface of the crêpe is dry and the edges slightly browned. Remove the pan from the heat, tip it over a large plate, and the crêpe should fall out. It is not necessary to cook both sides of the crêpe.

Return pan to heat and continue as above until all crêpe batter is used. Crêpes may be stacked one on top of the other.

Yield: 12 to 15 crêpes

Citrus Crêpes with Pineapple Cream

3 tablespoons plus 1½ teaspoons (52.5 ml) cornstarch
2 cups (500 ml) milk
3 egg yolks
6 ounces (175 ml) frozen unsweetened pineapple juice
concentrate, thawed
1 teaspoon (5 ml) vanilla extract
12 Citrus Crêpes (preceding recipe)
8 ounces (250 ml) canned unsweetened crushed
pineapple

Measure the cornstarch into a small saucepan. Dissolve it with a small amount of the milk, then stir in the remaining milk. Place over medium-low heat and cook, stirring constantly, until thickened, 3 to 4 minutes after mixture starts to boil. Remove from heat. Beat the egg yolks together with the juice concentrate. Stir into the thickened sauce. Return to heat and cook, stirring constantly, just until mixture begins to bubble. Do not let it boil; remove from heat. Stir in the vanilla and immediately cover with plastic wrap to prevent a skin forming on the surface. Cool, then refrigerate until serving time. The mixture will thicken even more upon standing.

To serve, spoon the cream mixture down the center of the crêpes and roll. Serve 2 crêpes per person. Spoon crushed pineapple over the top.

Serves 6

Crêpe Cake with Fruit and Cheese Filling

1 cup (225 g) ricotta cheese
½ cup (125 ml) unsweetened applesauce
½ teaspoon (2.5 ml) ground cinnamon
½ cup (75 g) raisins
12 Citrus Crêpes (page 77)
½ cup (50 g) chopped walnuts

In a small mixing bowl, combine the cheese, applesauce, cinnamon and raisins. Place 1 crêpe on a serving plate and spread it with about 2 tablespoons (30 ml) of the cheese mixture. Cover with another crêpe and spread it with some of the mixture. Continue layering and spreading until all the crêpes have been used and the last one is covered with cheese mixture. Sprinkle with the chopped walnuts. To serve, cut into wedges.

Serves 6

Stuffed Plums in Cream-Cheese Pastry

Cream-Cheese Pastry
1/3 cup (75 g) butter, at room temperature
1/3 cup (75 g) shortening
12 ounces (350 g) cream cheese, at room temperature
1/2 teaspoon (2.5 ml) vanilla extract
2 1/4 cups (270 g) flour
1/2 teaspoon (2.5 ml) salt

Filling
6 ripe plums, pitted
6 Brazil nuts, shelled

Cream butter, shortening and cream cheese until fluffy. Beat in the vanilla extract. Combine flour and salt; add in thirds to the cheese mixture, blending well after each addition. Form dough into a ball and chill.

Roll chilled dough out on a lightly floured surface to form a rectangle 12 x 18 inches (30 x 45 cm). Divide and cut the rectangle into 6 squares, 6 x 6 inches (15 x 15 cm) each.

Fill the cavity of each plum with a Brazil nut. Stand a stuffed plum upright in the center of each dough square. Bring the corners of pastry up to meet at the top of each plum, but do not seal the tips. Pinch the seams firmly together, leaving a hole at the top for steam to escape.

Place the pastries on an ungreased baking sheet, flattening the bottom of each one so that it will stand upright. Bake in a preheated 350°F. (180°C.) oven for 15 to 20 minutes, or until golden brown. Cool before serving.

Serves 6

Cream-Puff Pastry

¾ cup (175 ml) water
pinch of salt
6 tablespoons (90 g) butter
¾ cup (90 g) flour
3 eggs
½ teaspoon (2.5 ml) vanilla extract

Preheat oven to 400°F. (200°C.). Heat water, salt and butter to a full rolling boil in a saucepan. Reduce heat to low, and quickly dump in the flour all at once, mixing vigorously with a wooden spoon until the mixture leaves the sides of the pan and forms a ball. Remove from heat.

Beat in the eggs, one at a time, mixing until each addition is smooth and glossy. Add the vanilla, together with the last egg.

Drop dough by spoonfuls (depending on the desired size) onto a greased cookie sheet, 3 inches (7.5 cm) apart for large puffs or 1½ inches (4 cm) apart for small puffs. Bake in the preheated oven for 40 to 45 minutes for large puffs, or for about 20 minutes for small puffs. Turn off oven heat, remove puffs, and cut a small slit in each near the top. Return to warm oven and let stand for 5 or 10 minutes longer to allow puffs to dry inside. Cool on racks completely before filling.

Yield: 8 large puffs or 32 small puffs

Coconut Cream Puffs

Cream-Puff Pastry (page 81)
Fin de Nuit Cream (page 72)
½ cup (125 ml) freshly grated coconut
Chocolate Sauce (page 69)

Make 8 large cream puffs according to the recipe. When the puffs have cooled, make recipe for Fin de Nuit Cream; fold in the coconut. Slit cream puffs near top, and fill with the cream. Refrigerate until serving.

Prepare Chocolate Sauce, substituting Fin de Nuit for the Pedro Ximenez. Spoon cold sauce over each puff at time of serving.

Yield: 8 cream puffs

Pineapple Profiteroles with Chocolate Sauce

Cream-Puff Pastry (page 81)
2 teaspoons (5 g) unflavored gelatin
¼ cup (60 ml) cold water
6 ounces (175 ml) frozen unsweetened pineapple juice
  concentrate, thawed
½ cup (125 ml) heavy cream
8 ounces (225 g) canned unsweetened pineapple
  chunks
Chocolate Sauce (page 69)

Prepare 32 tiny cream puffs (profiteroles) according to the recipe. Cool puffs completely before filling.

Sprinkle the gelatin over the water in a heat-resistant cup and let stand for 5 minutes to soften. Set cup in a pan of very hot water, and allow to stand until gelatin is dissolved. Stir the dissolved gelatin into the juice concentrate. Cover and chill, stirring occasionally, until slightly thickened. Whip the cream until it stands in peaks; fold into the slightly thickened gelatin.

Make a slit in the top side of each profiterole. Spread slit apart and spoon in some of the pineapple filling. Chill filled profiteroles until serving time.

Prepare Chocolate Sauce, substituting pineapple juice concentrate for the apple juice concentrate. Chill.

To serve, mound profiteroles in a decorative serving dish. Drain pineapple chunks and place them decoratively in between the profiteroles as you build the mound. Spoon Chocolate Sauce over.

Serves 6 to 8

Orange Cream Éclairs

Cream-Puff Pastry (page 81)
2 eggs
6 ounces (175 ml) frozen unsweetened orange juice
  concentrate, thawed
4 tablespoons (60 ml) cornstarch
¼ cup (60 ml) cream sherry or Montilla Cream
2 cups (500 ml) milk, scalded
1 tablespoon (15 ml) grated orange rind
2 teaspoons (10 g) butter
1 teaspoon (5 ml) vanilla extract
Chocolate Sauce* (page 69)

Prepare dough for Cream-Puff Pastry. Force mixture through a pastry tube fitted with an éclair tip into finger shapes, about 4 inches (10 cm) long and 1 inch (2.5) cm) wide. Bake as for large cream puffs. Cool completely before filling.

In the top pan of a double broiler, beat the eggs with the juice concentrate. Measure the cornstarch into a small cup and gradually stir in the sherry until the mixture is smooth. Stir the mixture into the egg-concentrate mixture. Stir in the scalded milk and orange rind. Place pan over low heat, and cook while stirring constantly until mixture just comes to a boil. Place top pan over boiling water and continue to cook while stirring, until the mixture is thick, about 5 minutes. Remove from heat; stir in the butter. Cool slightly, stirring occasionally; stir in the vanilla. Transfer mixture to a bowl, cover tightly with plastic wrap, and chill.

To serve, cut a slit from one end to the other in the top part of each éclair. Fill with orange cream. Top each éclair with Chocolate Sauce.

Serves 10-12

---

*Prepare Chocolate Sauce by substituting cream sherry for the Pedro Ximenez and orange juice concentrate for the apple juice concentrate. Chill sauce.

Apple-Walnut Pie

pastry for 2-crust 9-inch (25-cm) pie
7 to 8 McIntosh, York or Cortland apples
2 tablespoons (15 g) whole-wheat flour
1 teaspoon (5 ml) ground cinnamon
pinch of ground nutmeg
2 tablespoons (30 ml) golden raisins
½ cup (50 g) chopped walnuts
¼ cup (60 ml) unsweetened apple juice
2 tablespoons (30 g) butter

Preheat oven to 400°F. (200°C). Line a 9-inch (25-cm) pie dish with half of the pastry.

Peel, core, and slice the apples. In a large mixing bowl, combine them with the next 6 ingredients, tossing until well mixed. Turn the apple mixture into the pastry shell and dot with the butter. Add the top crust, seal the edges, and cut a few gashes in the center for the steam to escape. Bake for 45 to 50 minutes, or until golden.

Serves 8

Blueberry Coconut-Cream Pie

½ cup (125 ml) frozen orange juice concentrate,
  thawed
1 tablespoon (15 ml) cornstarch
¼ teaspoon (1.5 ml) ground cinnamon
2 pints (450 g) blueberries, washed and picked over
1 baked and cooled pie shell, 9 inches (23 cm)
Coconut-Cream Topping (page 70)

Combine the juice concentrate, cornstarch and cinnamon in a small saucepan, and stir until smooth. Set over medium heat, bring to a boil, stirring constantly, and cook until thickened, about 1 minute. Add 1 pint (225 g) blueberries, and stir and cook for just a few seconds more. Remove from heat and cool.

Gently fold in the remaining pint of fresh blueberries. Turn mixture into the pie shell, cover, and chill until ready to serve. Top pie with Coconut-Cream Topping before serving.

Serves 6

Cranberry Nut Pie

pastry for 2-crust 9-inch (23-cm) pie
3 cups (750 ml) fresh cranberries
½ cup (50 g) chopped walnuts
3 tablespoons (45 ml) quick-cooking tapioca
6 ounces (175 ml) frozen unsweetened apple juice
  concentrate, thawed

Line a 9-inch (23-cm) pie plate with two thirds of the pastry. Preheat oven to 450°F. (230°C).

In a large bowl, combine the cranberries, cut into halves if desired, the walnuts, tapioca and concentrate; let stand for 15 minutes. Turn mixture into the lined pie plate; roll out remaining pastry and cover pie. Cut a few gashes in the top crust so that the steam can escape.

Bake for 10 minutes; reduce heat to 350°F. (180°C.) and bake for 30 minutes longer. Remove from oven, and cool on a wire rack for at least 2 hours before serving.

Serves 6 to 8

Macédoine Fruit Pie

½ pound (225 g) nectarines, sliced unpeeled
½ pound (225 g) sweet plums, halved and stoned
½ pound (225 g) seedless green grapes, halved
2 large navel oranges, peeled and sectioned
2 tablespoons (30 ml) apple or grape concentrate
2 tablespoons (30 ml) quick-cooking tapioca
¼ teaspoon (1.5 ml) ground cinnamon
¼ teaspoon (1.5 ml) ground nutmeg
pinch of salt
pastry for 2-crust 9-inch (23-cm) pie

Preheat oven to 400°F. (200°C.). In a large mixing bowl, combine the fruits with the fruit concentrate. Combine the dry ingredients in another bowl; then mix into the fruits. Let stand for 15 minutes.

Roll out half of the pastry and line a 9-inch (23-cm) pie dish. Roll out the remaining pastry to a rectangle 10 x 13 inches (25 x 33 cm); cut the rectangle into 6 lengthwise strips, each ½ inch (12 mm) wide. Place the fruit mixture in the prepared pie dish. Cover with the pastry strips, overlapping them in the center like the spokes of a wheel. Trim, seal, and flute the pastry edge; cover the edge with foil to prevent overbrowning. Place pie on a baking sheet to catch any spills and bake for 30 minutes. Reduce heat to 350°F. (180°C.) and bake for 30 minutes. Remove foil; bake for an additional 25 minutes, or until golden brown. Cool on a wire rack for at least 2 hours before serving.

Serves 6 to 8

Orange-Pear Pie

6 baking pears, cored and cut into bite-size pieces
2 navel oranges, peeled and sectioned
¼ cup (60 ml) frozen unsweetened orange juice
  concentrate, thawed
¼ cup (60 ml) water
2 tablespoons (30 ml) quick-cooking tapioca
½ teaspoon (2.5 ml) nutmeg
pastry for 2-crust 9-inch (23-cm) pie
½ cup (125 ml) chopped pecans

Preheat oven to 400°F. (200°C.). In a large mixing bowl, combine the pears, orange sections, juice concentrate, water, tapioca and nutmeg; let stand for 15 minutes.

Roll out half the pastry and line a 9-inch (23 cm) pie dish. Sprinkle the chopped pecans over the fitted pastry. Place the fruit mixture in the prepared pie dish. Roll out the remaining pastry and cut into strips. Arrange a lattice top crust over the pie. Trim, seal and flute the pastry edge. Cover the edge with foil to prevent over-browning. Place pie on a baking sheet to catch any spills and bake for 20 minutes. Reduce heat to 350°F. (180°C.), remove foil and bake for 30 minutes. Cool before serving.

Serves 6 to 8

Apricot Chess Tarts

pastry for 24 tart tins, 2½ inches across (6 cm)
6 ounces (175 g) cream cheese, at room temperature
1 pound (450 g) farmer or pot cheese, at room
*   temperature*
½ cup (125 ml) Apricot-Pineapple Preserves (page 75)
4 egg yolks
1 tablespoon (15 ml) grated orange rind
2 tablespoons (30 ml) sweet Marsala
24 pecan halves

Preheat oven to 450°F. (230°C.). Roll out dough and use to line 24 tart tins, 2½ inches across (6 cm). Bake blind (without filling) for 10 minutes, or until lightly browned. Set aside to cool. Reduce oven temperature to 350°F. (180°C.).

Beat cheeses and preserves together with an electric mixer until smooth; add egg yolks one at a time, beating after each addition. Beat in orange rind and Marsala.

Turn mixture into the tart shells, leaving a ¼-inch (6-mm) space at the top. Place tarts (still in their pans) on baking sheets; bake for 25 minutes, or until filling is lightly firm to touch. Cool and remove from pans. Top each tart with a pecan half.

Yield: 24 tarts

Glazed Grape and Brie Tart

(My favorite nickname for this dessert is "Froghead Pie.")

½ pound (225 g) ripe Brie cheese, chilled
3 ounces (90 g) cream cheese, at room temperature
2 tablespoons (30 g) butter, at room-temperature
½ cup (50 g) chopped walnuts
1 baked and cooled tart shell, 8 inch (20 cm)
2 cups (500 ml) sweet seedless green grapes
Wine Glaze* (page 70)

Remove the crust from the Brie while still cold (it will be easier to handle). Reserve the pieces of crust for another use. Place the Brie in a large mixing bowl, and let stand until of spreading consistency. Add the cream cheese and butter and beat the mixture until smooth and thoroughly mixed. Stir in the walnuts. Spread the cheese mixture over the bottom of the tart shell. Arrange the grapes, stem end down, all over the surface of the cheese. Spoon a generous amount of the Wine Glaze over the grapes. Chill before serving.

Serves 8

*If you like, stir ½ drop of green food coloring into the Wine Glaze.

Pumpkin Pie

pastry for 1-crust 9-inch (23-cm) pie
1 ½ cups (375 ml) unsweetened pumpkin purée
4 eggs, beaten
1 cup (250 ml) light cream or half-and-half
½ cup (125 ml) frozen unsweetened orange juice
  concentrate, thawed
½ cup (125 ml) Cresta Blanca Fin de Nuit
1 teaspoon (5 ml) ground cinnamon
½ teaspoon (2.5 ml) ground ginger
½ teaspoon (2.5 ml) ground nutmeg
Fin de Nuit Cream (page 72)

Preheat oven to 450°F. (230°C.). Line a 9-inch (23-cm) pie plate with the pastry, building up a fluted edge. In a large mixing bowl, beat together the pumpkin, eggs, light cream, juice concentrate, wine and spices. Pour into the prepared pie shell. Bake for 10 minutes. Reduce heat to 350°F. (180°C.). Bake for an additional 30 to 35 minutes, or until a knife inserted into the center comes out clean. Cool completely, then chill.

Prepare recipe for Fin de Nuit Cream. Use a decorating bag to pipe rosettes over the top of the pie. Chill until cream is set.

Serves 6 to 8

Glazed Strawberry Tart

Wine Glaze (page 70) or Golden Apple Glaze
  (page 71)
2 drops of red food coloring
6 ounces (175 g) cream cheese, at room temperature
½ cup (60 g) chopped almonds
1 baked and cooled tart shell 9 inches (23 cm)
1 quart (450 g) small fresh strawberries, hulled

Stir 2 drops of red food coloring into the Wine Glaze to give it a rosy glow. Place the cream cheese in a mixing bowl and beat it with an electric mixer or wooden spoon until fluffy. Add 2 tablespoons (30 ml) of the glaze and continue beating until blended. Fold in the almonds. Spread cream-cheese mixture over the bottom of the tart shell, cover, and chill for 30 minutes.

Arrange the strawberries, stem end down, over the top of the cheese mixture. Spoon glaze over to cover completely. Refrigerate until serving time.

Serves 6 to 8

French Fruit Tart

pastry for 1-crust 9-inch (23-cm) pie
Baked Orange Custard (page 50)
½ cup (125 ml) green seedless grapes
½ cup (125 ml) black or red grapes, seeded
1 small banana, peeled and sliced
1 navel orange, sectioned
1 pear, peeled, cored and cubed
Wine Glaze (page 70) or Golden Apple Glaze
(page 71)

Preheat oven to 400°F. (200°C.). Line a 9-inch (23-cm) pie plate with the pastry. Prepare recipe for Baked Orange Custard and turn the uncooked custard into the pie shell. Place on lower shelf of oven and bake for 15 minutes. Reduce heat to 325°F. (165°C.) and continue to bake for 20 to 25 minutes, until a metal skewer inserted into the center of the custard comes out clean. Remove from oven and cool on a wire rack.

When the pie is cool, prepare the fruits. Cut them directly into a bowl containing the Wine Glaze or Golden Apple Glaze. Toss gently to coat fruit. Mound the fruit on top of the cooled pie. Chill for at least 3 hours before serving.

Serves 8

Cakes and Cookies

Banana Sponge Roll
with Apricot-Pineapple Filling

1 large banana, peeled and quartered
3 eggs, separated
¼ cup (30 g) flour
¼ teaspoon (1.5 ml) baking powder
1 tablespoon (15 ml) apple concentrate
½ cup (50 g) finely ground almonds*
⅔ cup (150 ml) Apricot-Pineapple Preserves (page 75)

Preheat oven to 375°F. (190°C.); line a jelly-roll pan (13 x 9 inches, or 33 x 23 cm) with wax paper, greased on both sides.

Purée the banana with the egg yolks in a blender until smooth and fluffy. Blend in the flour and baking powder just until mixed.

Beat the egg whites until stiff; beat in the apple concentrate. Fold the banana mixture into the egg whites. Spread the mixture evenly in the prepared pan. Bake for 15 minutes, or until firm but springy to the touch.

Sprinkle a section (13 x 9 inches, or 33 x 23 cm) of a clean dish towel with the ground almonds. Remove cake from oven and immediately turn out onto the ground almonds. Carefully remove the wax paper. Using a sharp knife, cut off the stiff edges all around the cake. Spread the cake

*Shredded unsweetened coconut may be substituted for the ground almonds.

with a layer of preserves. Using the towel as an aid, roll the cake up tightly from the narrow end, jelly-roll fashion; remove the towel and set the cake aside, seam side down, to cool.

Yield: 9 slices, 1 inch (2.5 cm)

Variation: Cream and Fruit Filling

Omit the preserves. Sprinkle the unrolled cake with an additional ½ cup (50 g) finely ground almonds. Roll the cake in the towel and set aside to cool. Not more than 2 hours before serving, whip ½ cup (125 ml) heavy cream with 1 tablespoon (15 ml) apple or grape concentrate. Unroll the cooled cake and spread it with the whipped cream. Scatter fresh raspberries or sliced strawberries over the cream. Reroll the cake and chill, seam side down, until serving time.

Shortcake Dough

1 ½ cups (175 g) flour
¼ teaspoon (1.5 ml) salt
2 teaspoons (10 ml) baking powder
4 tablespoons (60 g) butter
1 tablespoon (15 ml) frozen unsweetened
*   apple juice concentrate, thawed*
melted butter
approximately ½ cup (125 ml) milk

Preheat oven to 400°F. (200°C.). Sift the flour, salt and baking powder into a large mixing bowl; cut into the butter, then rub between thumb and fingertips. Add the juice concentrate, then add enough milk, stirring quickly with a fork, to form a dough which is soft and light, but not sticky.

Turn dough out onto a lightly floured surface, and knead with floured hands for about 20 seconds, or until dough is smooth. Divide dough into 2 equal portions. Add more flour to the board, if necessary. With a floured rolling pin roll out each portion of the dough into a circle or rectangle about ½ inch (12 mm) thick.

Brush the top of each circle with melted butter. Place 1 circle on a baking sheet, buttered side up, and cover with the second circle, buttered side up. Bake for 15 to 20 minutes, or until risen and golden. Cool thoroughly before serving.

Individual shortcakes may be made by cutting the dough with floured cutter.

Serves 4 to 6

Strawberry Shortcake

1 Shortcake (preceding recipe)
1 quart (450 g) strawberries, hulled and halved
*¼ cup (60 ml), or more, frozen unsweetened apple
    juice concentrate, thawed*
½ cup (125 ml) heavy cream, whipped

Split the shortcake into 2 layers. Mix the strawberries with the juice concentrate, tossing to coat; additional concentrate may be used if desired. Place a generous amount of the berry mixture on top of the bottom cake layer; cover with the top layer. Pour remaining strawberries over the top and garnish with dollops of whipped cream. Serve immediately.

Serves 4 or 5

Note: Other berries or fruits may be substituted. Other flavors of juice concentrate may be substituted. Blackberries with apple juice concentrate is a delicious combination.

Dutch Apple Cake

Shortcake Dough (page 97)
1 egg, lightly beaten
4 York or Cortland apples
3 tablespoons (45 ml) frozen unsweetened apple juice
concentrate, thawed
½ teaspoon (2.5 ml) ground cinnamon
Sherry Sauce (page 73)

Preheat oven to 400°F. (200°C.). Butter an 8-inch (20-cm) square cake pan.

Prepare the recipe for Shortcake Dough, but add 1 egg with the ½ cup (125 ml) milk called for in the recipe, to make a soft dough. Spread the dough over the buttered cake pan.

Peel and core the apples, then cut each into 8 slices. Toss with the juice concentrate until coated. Arrange the apple slices overlapping in parallel rows on the dough. Sprinkle with the cinnamon. Bake for 30 minutes, or until cake tests done when a metal skewer inserted in the center comes out clean. Serve warm with Sherry Sauce.

Serves 6

Dark Chocolate Cake

2 ounces (60 g) unsweetened chocolate
½ cup (125 ml) shortening
6 ounces (175 ml) frozen unsweetened apple juice
   concentrate, thawed
2 eggs, lightly beaten
1 cup (120 g) all-purpose flour
¾ cup (120 g) whole wheat flour
½ teaspoon (2.5 ml) baking soda
½ teaspoon (2.5 ml) salt
1½ teaspoons (7.5 ml) baking powder
¾ cup (175 ml) milk
1 teaspoon (5 ml) vanilla extract

Preheat oven to 350°F. (180°C.). Grease a baking pan, 11 x 7 inches (28 x 18 cm); dust with whole wheat flour. Melt the chocolate in the top part of a double boiler over hot water. Remove from heat and beat in the shortening, juice concentrate and eggs. Sift the dry ingredients together, and tip the leftover flour back into the mixture. Alternately add the dry ingredients and the milk to the chocolate mixture. Beat in the vanilla. Turn the batter into the prepared pan and bake for 25 to 30 minutes, or until a metal skewer inserted in the center comes out clean. Cool slightly before serving or serve cold.

Serves 8

Note: This cake is delicious topped with Sherry Sauce, Spanish Orange Sauce, or Chocolate Sauce (recipes in sauce section).

Apple Walnut Cheesecake

1 cup (250 ml) packaged (plain) bread crumbs
1 cup (100 g) ground walnuts
½ teaspoon (2.5 ml) ground cinnamon
6 tablespoons (90 g) butter, melted
3 eggs, separated
6 ounces (175 ml) frozen unsweetened apple juice
  concentrate, thawed
¼ cup (60 ml) cream sherry or Montilla Cream
1 teaspoon (5 ml) vanilla extract
1 tablespoon (15 ml) grated lemon rind
1 cup (250 ml) heavy cream, whipped
¼ cup (30 g) sifted flour
1 pound (450 g) small-curd cottage cheese, sieved
8 to 10 perfect walnut halves

Mix crumbs, ground walnuts, cinnamon and butter smoothly. Press half of the mixture onto the bottom and partway up the sides of an 8-inch (20-cm) springform pan. Try to make a smooth lining. Chill in refrigerator for 1 hour. Set aside the remaining crumbs.

Preheat oven to 350°F. (180°C.). Beat the egg yolks until light and lemon-colored. Gradually beat in the juice concentrate, sherry and vanilla. Stir in the lemon rind. Fold the whipped cream into the yolk mixture. Beat the egg whites until they stand in peaks; fold them into the mixture. Mix the flour and sieved cottage cheese well; fold the cheese mixture into the yolk mixture.

Transfer the mixture to the springform pan. Sprinkle the remaining crumb mixture as evenly as possible over the top. Bake for 45 to 60 minutes, or until set. Press walnut halves gently into the top of the cake. Turn off oven heat and allow cake to remain in the oven for 30 minutes or longer, until the oven is cool. Cool cake, then chill in the refrigerator.

Serve cold. Run a sharp knife around the edges to loosen cake; remove springform.

Serves 8

Cherry-Almond Kolacky (co-*latch*-key)

(Polish Cookies)

1 recipe Cream-Cheese Pastry (page 80)
½ teaspoon (2.5 ml) almond extract
36 to 42 fresh sweet dark cherries
1 tablespoon (15 ml) frozen unsweetened orange juice
concentrate, thawed
36 to 42 large almond slivers

Prepare Cream-Cheese Pastry, substituting the almond extract for the vanilla extract. Chill the dough for 1½ to 2 hours, or until easy to handle. Preheat oven to 350°F. (180°C.). On a floured surface, roll the dough out to a thickness of ⅜ inch (9.5 mm). Cut out 2-inch (5-cm) circles or other small cookie shapes such as squares or ovals. Place on ungreased baking sheets. Make a "thumbprint" about ¼ inch (6 mm) deep in the center of each cookie.

Use a hairpin, or a cherry pitter, to pit the cherries, but do not cut them into halves. Place them in a bowl, add the juice concentrate and stir to coat. Place a slivered almond in the cavity of each cherry. Place a stuffed cherry into each thumbprint.

Bake for 10 to 15 minutes, or until lightly browned just around the edges. Be careful not to overbake as the bottoms will burn. Cool on a wire rack. If not to be eaten on the same day, place in a sealed or covered container in the refrigerator.

Yield: 36 to 42 cookies

Chocolate Coconut Cookies

1 cup (250 ml) unsweetened, grated coconut
1 egg yolk
3 tablespoons (45 ml) Chocolate Sauce (page 69)
2 egg whites

Preheat oven to 300 °F. (150 °C.). Stir the coconut, egg yolk and Chocolate Sauce together in a mixing bowl. Beat the egg whites until they stand in peaks. Fold the whites into the coconut mixture. Drop by spoonfuls onto a well-buttered cookie sheet, spacing them 1 inch (2.5 cm) apart. Bake for about 30 minutes, or until firm and beginning to brown. Remove from cookie sheet while still warm.

Yield: approximately 18

Macaroon Balls

1 cup (250 ml) unsweetened grated coconut
3 tablespoons (45 ml) Florio Almond Cream Marsala
1 large egg white, beaten

Preheat oven to 350 °F. (180 °C.). In a mixing bowl, stir the coconut with the Marsala to moisten evenly. Stir in the beaten egg white. Using your hands, form 1-inch (2.5-cm) balls. Place them on a well-buttered cookie sheet and bake for about 20 minutes, until they start to brown. Remove from the cookie sheet while still warm; cool on a wire rack.

Yield: approximately 12

Orange Oatmeal Cookies

¼ pound (120 g) butter, at room temperature
1 egg
6 ounces (175 ml) frozen unsweetened orange juice
  concentrate, thawed
1 cup (500 ml) flour
¼ teaspoon (1.5 ml) salt
1 teaspoon (5 ml) baking powder
1 cup (250 ml) rolled oats
½ cup (50 g) chopped walnuts
½ cup (85 g) golden raisins

Preheat oven to 350°F. (180°C.). Grease a cookie sheet with shortening.

Cream the butter and egg together until well mixed. Gradually beat in the juice concentrate. Combine the flour, salt, baking powder, oats, walnuts and raisins together in a large bowl; stir well. Stir the dry ingredients into the concentrate mixture. Drop by large teaspoons 2 inches (5 cm) apart onto the greased cookie sheet. Bake for 15 to 17 minutes, until lightly browned. Cool on a wire rack.

Yield: about 4 dozen

Orange-Raisin-Nut Cookies

½ cup (125 ml) frozen unsweetened orange juice
  concentrate, thawed
1 egg
¼ pound (120 g) butter, softened
2 cups (240 g) flour
2 teaspoons (10 ml) baking powder
½ teaspoon (2.5 ml) salt
½ teaspoon (2.5 ml) ground cinnamon
1 teaspoon (5 ml) grated orange rind
½ cup (85 g) raisins
½ cup (50 g) chopped walnuts

Preheat oven to 375°F. (190°C.). Beat concentrate with the egg and butter until combined. Mix in dry ingredients to form a batter, then stir in the fruit and nuts. Drop dough by tablespoons onto a greased cookie sheet, about 2 inches (5 cm) apart. Bake for 20 to 25 minutes, until lightly browned. Remove cookies from sheet while still warm, and let them cool on a wire rack.

Yield: approximately 30

Walnut Cups

6 ounces (175 g) cream cheese, at room temperature
6 tablespoons (90 g) butter, at room temperature
¼ teaspoon (1.5 ml) vanilla extract
1¼ cups (150 g) flour

Beat the cream cheese and butter together; beat in the vanilla. Gradually beat in the flour. Cover and chill dough until firm and easy to handle, 1 to 2 hours.

Place generous spoonfuls of dough into ungreased 1¾-inch (4.5-cm) muffin cups. Using floured fingers, press the dough against the sides and bottom so that each muffin cup is completely lined. Preheat oven to 325°F. (165°C.).

Filling

2 eggs, beaten
¼ cup (60 ml) frozen unsweetened orange juice
    concentrate, thawed
2 tablespoons (30 g) butter, melted
1 cup (100 g) chopped walnuts
¼ cup (60 ml) finely chopped pressed dates

Mix filling ingredients together in a bowl. Fill the lined muffin cups with the mixture. Bake for 25 to 30 minutes. Cool slightly, then remove from pans.

Yield: about 3 dozen

Basically Fruits

Avocado Dessert

6 ounces (175 ml) frozen unsweetened
  pineapple juice concentrate, thawed, but chilled
2 tablespoons (30 ml) white port
3 large avocados, chilled
lemon juice

Combine the cold juice concentrate and the white port in a small mixing bowl. Halve and pit the avocados, and sprinkle them with lemon juice to prevent browning. Place about 2 tablespoons (30 ml) of the concentrate-port mixture into each avocado cavity. Serve immediately.

Serves 6

Chocolate-Dipped Strawberries

1 quart (450 g) fresh strawberries, chilled, washed and
  hulled
Chocolate Sauce, double recipe (page 69)

Prepare the sauce so that it can chill for at least 3 hours before serving. Divide the cold sauce equally among 6 demitasse cups. Place each cup in the center of a dessert plate and surround it with berries. Set out small fruit forks so that the berries can be pierced and dunked.

Serves 6

Seasonal Ambrosias

fruit as selected for the season
1 cup (250 ml) freshly shredded coconut
¼ cup (60 ml) frozen unsweetened orange juice
*   concentrate, thawed*
½ cup (125 ml) sweet white table wine (see page 14
*   and pages 151-168)*

Arrange alternating layers of fruits and coconut in a transparent glass serving bowl. Combine the juice concentrate and wine and pour over the fruit. Cover and chill until serving time.

Serves 8

Spring
1 quart (450 g) strawberries, hulled and halved
1 ripe pineapple, flesh cut into cubes

Summer
6 nectarines, halved, pitted and sliced
6 plums, halved, pitted and sliced
1 pound (450 g) seedless green grapes

Fall
5 kiwi fruits, peeled and sliced
4 Golden Delicious apples, cored and sliced
1 pomegranate, use only the pulpy red seeds

Winter
5 navel oranges, segmented
3 small or 2 large seedless pink grapefruits,
*   segmented*

Baked Apples with Wine

6 York or other baking apples, cored
¾ cup (175 ml) chopped, pressed dates
¾ cup (75 g) chopped walnuts
3 tablespoons (45 g) butter, melted
Mirassou Fleuri Blanc or other sweet white
    table wine

Preheat oven to 375°F. (190°C.). Butter and lightly flour the bottom of a baking dish that will hold the apples comfortably without being too large. Pare a wide band of skin from the stem end of each apple and arrange the apples in the baking dish, pared end up. Combine the dates and walnuts in a mixing bowl, and pour the melted butter over them, tossing to coat. Stuff the apple cavities with this mixture. Pour a ¼-inch (6-mm) layer of wine gently over the apples and into the dish. Bake uncovered, basting 3 or 4 times with the wine, for about 30 minutes, or until a wooden pick or metal skewer can easily pierce the center of the apples. Serve warm with the pan juices.

Serves 6

Apricot Chantilly

½ pound (225 g) sun-dried apricots
2 cups (500 ml) boiling water
¼ cup (60 ml) frozen unsweetened orange
*   juice concentrate*
1½ teaspoons (7.5 ml) vanilla extract
1 cup (250 ml) heavy cream
¼ cup (25 g) chopped walnuts
3 teaspoons (15 ml) freeze-dried coffee

Place the apricots in a heat-resistant bowl and pour the boiling water over them; cover and let stand at room temperature for several hours or overnight.

Drain the apricots and purée them with the juice concentrate and vanilla extract in a blender. Whip the cream until it stands in stiff peaks. Fold in the walnuts and apricot purée.

Spoon equal amounts of the mixture into 6 custard cups or, for a formal occasion, into 6 large balloon wineglasses. Chill for 1 hour. Sprinkle each portion with ½ teaspoon (2.5 ml) freeze-dried coffee before serving.

Serves 6

Bananas Marsala

3 large, semiripe bananas
4 tablespoons (60 g) butter
1 teaspoon (5 ml) cornstarch
¼ cup (60 ml) water
½ cup (125 ml) sweet Marsala or Florio Almond
  Cream Marsala
shredded fresh coconut

Peel bananas, cut lengthwise into halves, and fry quickly turning once in the butter, until golden. Dissolve the cornstarch in the water and combine with the Marsala. Pour liquid over the bananas, bring to a boil, lower heat, and simmer gently for about 5 minutes, until the bananas are tender. Serve hot, sprinkled with shredded coconut.

Serves 3 or 6

Stuffed Cantaloupe

3 ripe cantaloupes
1 pint (225 g) raspberries
2 cups (500 ml) seedless green grapes
¼ cup (60 ml) sweet white table wine
¼ cup (60 ml) frozen unsweetened orange juice
  concentrate, thawed

Shortly before serving, halve the melons and remove the seeds. Pick over and wash the raspberries and grapes; place them in a bowl. Combine the wine and juice concentrate and mix well. Pour over the berries and grapes, gently tossing to coat. Fill melon cavities with the berry-grape mixture. Serve cold.

Serves 6

Cherry Fool

1 ¼ pounds (565 g) fresh sweet cherries
3 tablespoons (45 ml) Florio Almond Cream Marsala
1 tablespoon (15 ml) arrowroot
pinch of ground cinnamon
⅔ cup (150 ml) water
1 cup (250 ml) heavy cream

Reserve 6 perfect cherries with their stems for garnish. Working over a bowl, halve and pit the remaining cherries. Stir the Marsala into the cherries; set aside.

Place the arrowroot and cinnamon in a small saucepan. Gradually stir in the water until the mixture is smooth. Place over medium-low heat and cook, stirring constantly, until mixture comes to a boil and thickens. Remove from heat; stir in the Marsala and cherries. Cover and chill.

Just before serving, beat the heavy cream until it stands in peaks. Partially fold the cream into the chilled fruit mixture; it should appear streaky. Spoon the mixture into dessert goblets or large balloon wineglasses. Top each portion with a reserved cherry for garnish. Serve immediately.

Serves 6

Baked Figs

24 dried figs
6 tablespoons (90 ml) cream sherry or Montilla Cream
2-inch (5-cm) strip of orange peel
boiling water

Preheat oven to 275°F. (140°C.). Arrange the figs in a shallow casserole dish. Add the sherry and orange peel. Pour on just enough boiling water to cover the figs. Bake for 1½ to 2 hours, or until the figs are plumped. Cool and chill. Discard the orange peel. Serve cold with cream.

Serves 6

Broiled Grapefruit

For each serving:
½ large pink grapefruit
1 tablespoon (15 ml) Cresta Blanca Fin de Nuit, cream
  sherry or Cream Montilla

Prepare the halves for serving: Remove seeds, loosen the sections (sides and edge) with a sharp knife, remove center core and dividing membrane. Sprinkle each section with wine. Slide under a preheated broiler and broil 3 to 4 inches (7.5 to 10 cm) from the source of heat for 12 to 15 minutes. The edge of the skin should just begin to brown, and the fruit should be warm throughout. Serve hot.

Glazed Citrus Cup

3 large pink grapefruits
2 navel oranges
6 ounces (175 ml) frozen unsweetened pineapple-
  orange juice concentrate, thawed
2 tablespoons (30 ml) cream sherry or Montilla Cream
shredded fresh coconut

Cut the grapefruits into halves. Cut around the edges and lift out the insides of the fruit. Reserve the shells. Section the halved grapefruits into a bowl, discarding the membranes. Peel and section the oranges. Cut the sections into halves if they are very large; add to the grapefruit sections.

Place the juice concentrate in a small metal saucepan. Bring to a rapid boil, stirring constantly, and cook until the concentrate reduces slightly and begins to turn golden. Remove from heat; cool slightly. Stir in the sherry or Montilla. Pour mixture over the fruit and toss gently to coat. Chill until serving time.

Shortly before serving, spoon fruit mixture into the 6 reserved grapefruit shells. Sprinkle with shredded coconut. Serve chilled.

Serves 6

Best Dressed Winter Fruit Cups

4 navel oranges
2 cups (500 ml) dairy sour cream or plain yogurt
⅓ cup (90 ml) frozen unsweetened orange juice
  concentrate, thawed
½ teaspoon (2.5 ml) ground ginger
5 kiwi fruits

Grate 1 tablespoon (15 ml) rind from one of the oranges. Combine rind, sour cream, juice concentrate and ginger in a small mixing bowl, and stir until thoroughly mixed. Cover and refrigerate.

Peel and section the 4 oranges. Peel and slice the kiwi fruits into rounds. Combine the orange sections and kiwi slices, tossing gently in another small mixing bowl. Cover and refrigerate.

To serve, spooon the fruit mixture into 6 individual dessert dishes or large balloon wineglasses; pour a portion of sauce over each.

Serves 6

Red Fruit Compote

1 pound (450 g) plums, halved and stoned
1 pound (450 g) Bing cherries, halved and pitted
½ cup (125 ml) ruby port
¼ cup (60 ml) water
1 quart (450 g) raspberries, divided
½ cup (125 ml) heavy cream, whipped
cinnamon

Place the plums, cherries, wine and water in a saucepan. Bring to a boil, reduce heat, and simmer gently for 20 to 25 minutes, until the mixture is soft and pulpy. Set aside 18 perfect raspberries for garnish; add remaining berries to the compote and cook for an additional 5 minutes. Cool slightly and serve warm, or chill in the refrigerator. Serve with a dollop of whipped cream, lightly sprinkled with cinnamon and garnished with the reserved raspberries.

Serves 6 to 8

Sparkling Fruit Cup

This delightful dessert is especially suitable for weddings and New Year's celebrations.

2 cups (500 ml) mixed fresh fruits
Asti Spumante

Choose fruits that are plentiful for the season—small berries (raspberries, blueberries), halved strawberries, cubed peaches, nectarines, plums, papaya or melon, kiwi fruit (sliced and halved), small seedless grapes, pineapple tidbits, etc. Combine 2 or 3 fruits contrasting in color; Make sure they are small, or cut them into small bite-size pieces. Cover and refrigerate the mixture until serving time.

To serve, half-fill large balloon wineglasses with chilled Asti Spumante. Float generous spoonfuls of the mixed fruit in the wine. Serve immediately.

Serves 6 to 8

Melon Bowl Medley

1 large honeydew melon
1 pint (225 g) strawberries, hulled and halved
1 pint (225 g) blueberries, stems removed
½ cup (125 ml) French Sauternes or Barsac or other
  sweet golden table wine

Choose a ripe melon with an unblemished skin. Cut a lid from the top of the melon, using a decorative zig-zag motion. Set the lid aside and scoop out the seeds. Make a sturdy wreath from crumpled aluminum foil; use this as a nest for the melon base so that it will stand straight and upright. Using a melon-ball cutter or a small spoon, remove the flesh and place it in a large mixing bowl as you work along. Be careful not to puncture a hole in the sides or through the bottom of the melon. Replace the lid on the melon shell and store it in the refrigerator.

Add the strawberries, blueberries and wine to the melon balls and toss until well mixed. Cover and chill in the refrigerator.

When ready to serve, transfer the fruit mixture with its juices to the hollowed melon shell. Fill it so that the fruit forms a slight mound at the top of the melon. Replace the lid at an angle so that the fruit is peeping out; secure lid with a wooden pick, if necessary.

Serves 8

Minted Melon Mélange

12 fresh mint leaves
pinch of salt
⅓ cup (90 ml) frozen unsweetened apple juice
*   concentrate, thawed*
3 cups (750 ml) mixed melon balls or cubes*

The day before serving, place the mint leaves in a cup together with the salt, and use scissor points to mince finely. Stir the juice concentrate into the chopped leaves, cover, and let steep in the refrigerator overnight.

To serve, place the melon balls in a decorative serving bowl. Strain the juice concentrate through a fine sieve and drizzle it over the melon balls; toss to coat them with the sauce. Garnish with additional mint leaves. Serve chilled.

Serves 6

*Watermelon, honeydew and cantaloupe make an attractive mixture.

Glazed Oranges

6 large navel oranges
6 ounces (175 ml) frozen unsweetened pineapple-
  orange juice concentrate, thawed

Using a potato peeler, thinly pare the rind from 1 orange. Use a sharp knife to cut the rind into shreds.

Place the juice concentrate and the orange-rind shreds in a small metal saucepan. Place over medium heat and bring to a rapid boil, stirring constantly. Cook until the mixture begins to brown; do not let it burn. Remove from heat. The concentrate will have reduced itself during the cooking, and will be slightly thick. Cool.

Peel the oranges over a bowl, using a sharp knife. Remove all white pith. Cut the oranges into ½-inch (12-mm) slices across the segments. Reshape each orange after cutting it by spearing the slices with a toothpick or two. Arrange the whole, reshaped oranges in a large, decorative dessert bowl. Pour the cooled concentrate and shredded rind over the fruit. Cover and chill until serving time.

Serves 6

Baked Stuffed Peaches or Nectarines

6 ripe freestone peaches or nectarines
¾ cup (130 g) golden raisins, chopped
¾ cup (75 g) chopped walnuts
3 tablespoons (45 g) butter, melted
cream sherry or Montilla Cream

Preheat oven to 350°F. (180°C.). Butter and lightly flour the bottom of a large baking dish. Cut the fruit into halves, remove and discard the stones, and arrange cut side up in the baking dish. Combine the raisins and walnuts in a mixing bowl; pour the melted butter over and toss to coat. Stuff the cavities of the fruit with this mixture. Gently pour the wine over the fruit and into the dish to the depth of about ¼ inch (6 mm). Bake for about 20 minutes, until tender, basting occasionally. Serve warm with the pan juices.

Serves 6

Baked Almond Pears

6 firm pears, halved, with cores removed
½ cup (60 g) chopped almonds
2 tablespoons (30 g) butter, melted
¾ cup (175 ml) Florio Almond Cream Marsala

Preheat oven to 350°F. (180°C.). Arrange the pear halves cut side up in a buttered baking dish. Stir the butter into the almonds and use to fill the pear cavities. Gently pour the Marsala over the pears. Bake for 30 minutes, basting occasionally. Serve warm or cold.

Serves 6

Roquefort Pears with Sauternes

6 large firm pears
2 cups (500 ml) French Sauternes
2 tablespoons (30 ml) cornstarch
¼ cup (60 ml) water
4 ounces (120 g) cream cheese, at room temperature
4 ounces (120 g) Roquefort cheese, at room
    temperature
2 teaspoons (10 ml) grated lemon rind

Peel, halve, and core pears. Pour the Sauternes into a shallow pan and bring to a boil. Add half of the pears; simmer, basting with wine, turning as needed, until fork-tender, about 8 minutes. Carefully remove cooked pears to a shallow dish, and cook the remaining pears. Transfer them to the shallow dish.

Dissolve the cornstarch in the water. Add to the wine and cook, stirring, until thickened. Pour the sauce over the pears and let stand until cool. Chill in the refrigerator for several hours.

Combine the cheeses with 2 to 3 tablespoons (30 to 45 ml) of the pear syrup. Add the lemon rind and beat until smooth and fluffy. Drain pears and put the halves together with the cheese mixture inside, so that they once again appear whole. Arrange them standing up in a serving dish and pour the wine sauce over.

Serves 6

Spiced Pears in Port Wine

6 large firm pears
1½ cups (350 ml) ruby port
½ cup (125 ml) frozen unsweetened apple juice
concentrate, thawed
5 whole cloves
2-inch (5-cm) cinnamon stick

Thinly peel the pears, keeping them whole. Leave the stalk and core intact. Place the peeled pears on their sides in a shallow, wide saucepan. Combine the port and the juice concentrate and pour the mixture over the pears; add the cloves and cinnamon stick. Bring the liquid to a boil, reduce the heat, cover, and simmer gently for 30 to 40 minutes, or until pears are tender. Midway through cooking, carefully turn the pears and add more wine, if necessary.

Place the pears in a serving bowl, remove the spices from the wine, and pour it over the pears. Cool, cover with plastic wrap, and chill in the refrigerator until serving time. Serve cold.

Serves 6

Pineapple-Avocado Boats

1 small pineapple, flesh cut into small cubes
3 avocados, chilled
lemon juice
6 ounces (175 ml) frozen unsweetened pineapple juice
concentrate, thawed, but chilled
6 tablespoons (90 ml) shredded fresh coconut

Place the pineapple cubes in a mixing bowl, cover, and refrigerate until chilled. Halve and pit the avocados; using a teaspoon, scoop out the flesh in chunks, adding them to the pineapple as you work along. Be careful not to puncture the rinds. Sprinkle a small amount of lemon juice over the avocado chunks, then toss gently to combine with the pineapple.

Mound the fruit mixture into the 6 avocado shells and drizzle each portion with 2 tablespoons (30 ml) of the juice concentrate. Top each boat with 1 tablespoon (15 ml) shredded coconut. Serve immediately.

Serves 6

Ported Strawberries and Nectarine Dessert

1 quart (450 g) fresh strawberries, hulled and crushed
½ cup (125 ml) ruby port
3 large freestone nectarines
6 ounces (175 g) cream cheese, softened
¼ cup (60 ml) light cream or half-and-half

Combine the strawberries and port in a bowl, cover, and chill until serving time. Halve and pit the nectarines; place one half in each of 6 dessert bowls. Spoon the strawberries over.

Beat the cream cheese until fluffy and gradually beat in the cream. Continue beating until smooth. Spoon over the fruit or serve separately as a topping.

Serves 6

Strawberries Romanoff

1 pint (225 g) fresh strawberries
3 tablespoons (45 ml) frozen unsweetened orange
juice concentrate, thawed
1 small juice orange
2 teaspoons (5 g) unflavored gelatin
1 cup (250 ml) heavy cream

Hull and lightly crush the strawberries; stir in the juice concentrate. Finely grate the orange rind (do not include any of the white pith) and add to the strawberries. Cut the orange into halves and squeeze the juice into a heat-resistant cup. Sprinkle the gelatin over the juice and let stand for 5 minutes to soften. Set the cup in a pan of very hot water and gently stir until the gelatin dissolves. Use a rubber spatula to scrape the dissolved gelatin into the strawberry mixture; stir well. Chill until slightly thickened.

Whip the cream until it stands in peaks. Fold the whipped cream into the strawberry mixture. Spoon into 4 dessert dishes or balloon wineglasses. Chill for 1 hour before serving.

Serves 4

Summer Fool

1 quart (450 g) fresh strawberries, hulled
¼ cup (60 ml) frozen unsweetened orange juice
  concentrate, thawed
2 tablespoons (30 ml) arrowroot
1 pint (225 g) fresh raspberries
1 cup (250 ml) heavy cream

Mash the strawberries with a fork until they make a coarse purée. Measure out 1 cup (250 ml) of the mashed berries into a small saucepan. In a cup, stir the juice concentrate into the arrowroot until arrowroot is dissolved and no lumps remain. Stir the arrowroot mixture into the saucepan containing the berries; bring to a boil, stirring constantly, and cook until the sauce is thick and clear. Remove from heat, transfer the mixture to a bowl, and allow to cool slightly. Add the remaining mashed strawberries, and stir to mix well. Select 18 perfect raspberries for garnish; set aside in the refrigerator. Stir the remaining raspberries into the strawberry mixture. Cover and chill.

Shortly before serving, whip the heavy cream until it stands in stiff peaks. Partially fold the cream (not too thoroughly) into the chilled berry sauce; the mixture should appear streaky. Spoon the fool into individual dessert goblets or balloon wineglasses; top each with 2 or 3 of the reserved raspberries. Serve immediately.

Serves 6 to 8

Summer Zabaglione

1 pint (225 g) fresh strawberries
1 pint (225 g) fresh raspberries
5 egg yolks
½ cup (125 ml) sweet Marsala or Florio Almond Cream
  Marsala

Reserve 6 to 8 whole strawberries; hull and halve the remaining strawberries. Toss strawberry halves with the raspberries in a mixing bowl. Divide berry mixture among 6 to 8 large balloon wineglasses; cover them and refrigerate.

In the top part of a double boiler, combine egg yolks and Marsala. Cook over very hot, but not boiling, water, beating constantly, for about 10 minutes, until thickened. Spoon zabaglione over the berries; garnish each portion with a reserved whole strawberry; serve immediately.

Serves 6 to 8

Yogurt Fruit Parfaits

1 ½ teaspoons (7.5 ml) cornstarch
6 ounces (175 ml) frozen unsweetened pineapple juice
concentrate, thawed
2 egg yolks, lightly beaten
8 ounces (250 ml) plain yogurt
1 cup (250 ml) heavy cream
1 cup (250 ml) chopped nuts
3 papayas, peeled, seeded and diced
3 pears, cut into bite-size pieces
1 ½ cups (375 ml) seeded black grapes

In a saucepan, combine the cornstarch and juice concentrate, stirring until smooth. Bring to a boil and cook for 2 minutes while constantly stirring. Temper the egg yolks with a small amount of the hot syrup, then beat the yolks into the remaining syrup. Return to heat and cook, stirring just until mixture begins to boil. Remove from heat. In a mixing bowl, stir hot mixture into yogurt. Cool to room temperature, stirring occasionally. Whip the cream until it stands in peaks. Fold cream into the cooled mixture. Cover and chill.

To assemble, arrange alternating layers of the yogurt mixture with the nuts and fruits in individual parfait or sherbet glasses, ending with the nuts.

Serves 6

Glazed Fruit Compote with Custard

For the Custard:
2 cups (500 ml) half-and-half or light cream
3 eggs, lightly beaten
¼ cup (60 ml) frozen unsweetened orange juice
*   concentrate, thawed*
2 tablespoons (30 ml) sweet or cream sherry

For the Glazed Fruit:
3 navel oranges
4 tablespoons (60 ml) butter
¼ cup (60 ml) frozen unsweetened orange juice
*   concentrate, thawed*
¼ teaspoon (1.5 ml) ground cinnamon
3 large bananas, cut into 2-inch (5-cm) chunks

In a medium-sized saucepan, use a wire whisk to combine half-and-half, eggs and juice concentrate. Cook, constantly stirring, over low heat until mixture thickens and coats the back of a metal spoon. Remove from heat. Stir in the sherry. Spoon custard into 6 8-ounce (250-ml) goblets or dessert dishes. Cover and refrigerate until well chilled.

Grate 2 tablespoons (30 ml) of peel from one orange and set aside. Remove peel from the oranges. Cut fruit into ½-inch (13-mm) slices.

In a skillet over low heat, melt the butter. Add the concentrate and cinnamon and cook until bubbly. Add the bananas and oranges and cook for 5 minutes, or until heated through. Sprinkle with the grated orange peel and gently turn the mixture in the pan. Serve the hot fruit over the chilled custard.

Serves 6

Confections

Concord-Persimmon Fruit Leather

Because of its sweet taste and chewy texture, this leather makes a delightful snack or substitute for candy. It may also be cut into small decorative shapes and used as a dipper with sour cream or yogurt. Alternatively, chop it into small pieces and use it in place of raisins or candied fruits in baking.

Place an oven thermometer in the center of the middle shelf of your oven, prop the door open, and check the reading after about 15 minutes. The oven must be preheated to between 120°F. (50°C.) and 150°F. (65°C.). The heat from the pilot light or the bulb should be adequate. If necessary, try raising or lowering the oven shelf until the desired reading is obtained; opening the oven door at different levels may also help. The door must remain open at least 1 inch (2.5 cm) to allow moisture to escape while the fruit is drying. The temperature control is very important, so experiment before attempting leather drying.

> 3 cups (750 ml) Concord grapes, stemmed and washed
> 2 ripe persimmons, washed, stems and caps removed,
>   then halved
> ¼ teaspoon (1.5 ml) ground cinnamon
> ⅛ teaspoon (.5 ml) ground ginger
> ⅛ teaspoon (.5 ml) ground allspice

Place the fruits in the top part of a double boiler; cover and cook over boiling water for 20 minutes, until soft. Press fruits through a food mill to remove seeds. Pick out as many of the skins as possible from the mill and return them to the purée. Place in a blender and process until mixture is smooth and the skins are well torn. Blend in the spices.

Line a jelly-roll pan 11 x 15 inches (28 x 38 cm) with plastic wrap. (Do not use aluminum foil or wax paper.) Wet or tape the edges of the baking sheet to hold the wrap in place. Pour the fruit mixture onto the prepared pan and spread evenly. Place pan in preheated oven and dry for 6 to 24 hours. (Several factors affect the drying time.) Check the leather as it dries, and rotate the pan for even drying. Test by separating the dried fruit from the wrap. Leather is done when it easily pulls away from the plastic film without breaking and leaves no sticky spots. Brittle leather is a sign of overdrying, so testing is a must.

Remove from pan while still warm. Place the leather on a clean piece of plastic wrap and roll, like a jelly roll, together with the wrap; the wrap will keep the leather from sticking together. Tightly wrap in double freezer bags or triple plastic bags (one inside the other) and then in aluminum foil. Store in the freezer or at room temperature, in a dark place. Leather will keep for up to 1 year.

Apple-Apricot Fruit Leather

2 cups (500 ml) unsweetened applesauce
2 jars 4¾ ounces each, unsweetened
    apricot baby food purée
¼ teaspoon (1.5 ml) ground cinnamon

Thoroughly combine all ingredients. Preheat oven and prepare jelly-roll pan. Follow drying instructions as directed for Concord-Persimmon Fruit Leather.

Tropical Chips

2 firm, ripe bananas
frozen unsweetened pineapple juice concentrate,
    thawed
finely grated fresh coconut

Preheat the oven and prepare a jelly-roll pan as directed in the recipe for Concord-Persimmon Fruit Leather.

Peel the bananas and cut them evenly into slices ¼-inch (6-mm) thick. Dip the slices into the pineapple concentrate, then into the grated coconut. Place on the lined jelly-roll pan. Dry in oven with slightly open door at 120°F. (50°C.) to 150°F. (65°C.).

Eat the chips plain as a sweet snack or dip them into yogurt or sour cream. The chips should be stored in an airtight container at room temperature.

Fruit and Nut Balls

1 cup (250 ml) dried figs, stems removed
¾ cup (130 g) raisins
1 cup (250 ml) sun-dried apricots or pitted pressed
    dates
1 cup (250 ml) chopped walnuts
¼ cup (60 ml) unsweetened grated coconut

Using a meat grinder fitted with a fine blade, alternately grind the fruits and walnuts so that they come out mixed. Shape the mixture into small balls with your hands. Gently shake the balls in a bag containing the coconut.

Yield: 30 balls

Stuffed Prunes or Dates

Remove the pits from a quantity of prunes or pressed dates. Stuff the cavities with peanut butter; then dab the peanut side in unsweetened grated coconut.

Stuffed Apricots

Stir a small amount of cream sherry or other fortified wine into cream cheese until it is soft enough to be forced through a pastry tube. Fill a decorating bag with the mixture and pipe it onto the cavities of sun-dried apricots. Top each with a whole almond or a walnut or pecan half. Refrigerate until serving.

Stuffed Grapes

Cut partway through Tokay, Emperor or Concord grapes and remove the pips. Combine equal portions of cream cheese and blue-veined cheese such as Roquefort, Gorgonzola, etc. Thin with a little milk, if necessary, and fill a decorating bag with the mixture. Pipe mixture into the grape cavities. Place stuffed grapes on a plate or tray lined with grape leaves. Refrigerate until serving.

Jams
and Jellies

JAMS and jellies have become a staple product in most American homes. Unfortunately, they are always over-loaded with vast amounts of sugar (that's why we all like them so much!), and even those dietetic simulations in the special diet section of the supermarket are sweetened with saccharin. Up until now, even homemade jams and jellies have required the use of large quantities of sugar, not only for flavor but also to help them jell.

I am very pleased to bring your attention to a wonderful new product called "Slim Set"* for making homemade jams and jellies without the use of sugar or saccharin. This product can be found in your supermarket in the section where you normally find Certo, and other aids to jelly-making. "Slim Set" was test-marketed for 3 years and demonstrated beyond doubt that it could make jams and jellies of excellent quality. Complete instructions are included in the package, using small amounts of honey as the sweetening ingredient. Pure honey, of course, is a wonderful sweetener, but it does have a very distinct flavor. As an alternative to honey, I suggest trying the recipes in this book using frozen juice concentrates for a wider variety of sweetening flavors.

*At this writing, "Slim Set" is the only such product on the market. Other, similar ones, may follow, and I am not implying an endorsement of this over future competitors.

Jams with Slim Set

Measure 3 cups (750 ml) of fruit pulp, prepared as directed, without sweeteners, into a 3- to 4-quart (3- to 4-liter) kettle. It may be necessary to add a specified amount of lemon juice, depending on the fruit, when preparing it, and manufacturer's instructions will indicate this. Add ¼ cup (60 ml) frozen unsweetened juice concentrate, of any flavor, thawed. Add ¾ cup (175 ml) water; stir and taste for sweetness. If a sweeter jam is desired, add up to 2 tablespoons (30 ml) more of juice concentrate. Add 1 package 1¾ ounces (50 g) Slim Set and whisk to dissolve and combine ingredients thoroughly. Place kettle over high heat, bring to a boil, and boil rapidly for 2 minutes, stirring constantly. Remove from heat; skim foam. Immediately pour into prepared jam jars, leaving a ½-inch (12-mm) space at the top for a paraffin seal or ⅛-inch (3-mm) space for a two-piece metal lid. Follow manufacturer's instructions for sealing and storing containers.

Yield: 3½ cups (875 ml)

Jellies with Slim Set

Measure 3¾ cups (900 ml) of unsweetened fruit juice into a 3- or 4-quart (3- or 4-liter) kettle. If preparing juice from scratch, follow manufacturer's directions, adding lemon juice where required, but omitting any sweeteners. Add ¼ cup (60 ml) of any flavor thawed unsweetened juice concentrate. If a sweeter jelly is desired, add up to 2 tablespoons (30 ml) more of concentrate. Add 1 package (1¾ ounces or 50 g) Slim Set and whisk firmly to dissolve and combine ingredients thoroughly. Place kettle over high heat, bring to a boil, and boil rapidly, stirring constantly for 1 minute. Remove from heat; skim foam. Follow manufacturer's directions thereafter.

Yield: 3¾ cups (900 ml)

Fruit
Buying Guide

APPLES Select firm apples that have a bright, clean skin color. Well-colored apples are an indication of full flavor. Apples picked immature often lack color and flavor. Check for bruises, which lead to rapid decay. Larger apples are more likely to be overripe, especially toward the end of the season, than smaller fruit. Overripe fruit will have a dry, mealy texture. Apples like cold temperatures and should be refrigerated in the produce drawer or in sealed plastic bags to prevent dehydrating.

Apples are grown commercially in 34 states and are available all through the year. The best season, however, is from September through November, when they are being harvested. At other times, most available apples will have come from cold storage.

Many varieties are available, but the best for sugarless cookery are these:

RED DELICIOUS, *September to May; red, crisp, sweet eating apple, best used raw.*

GOLDEN DELICIOUS, *October to June; yellow, crisp, sweet eating apple, best used raw. Raw slices do not turn brown when exposed to air.*

McINTOSH, *October to May; two-toned green and red skin, juicy, crisp, medium-sweet, all-purpose apple. Requires shorter cooking time than other varieties.*

CORTLAND, October to January; bright red, crisp, sweet, all-purpose apple. Raw slices do not turn brown when exposed to air.

YORK, October to March; light red with russet markings, crisp, sweet apple that holds its shape and flavor when cooked. Very good apple for baking.

APRICOTS Since this fruit is very fragile, it is usually picked underripe. Succulent, tree-ripened fruit cannot be shipped and is found only in the growing areas (California, Utah and Washington). Good-quality fruit is plump, uniformly deep gold or yellow-orange, and juicy. Although firm, it should yield just slightly under pressure. Immature fruit is greenish in color and hard, while old fruit is pale, soft and sometimes shriveled. Nearly ripe fruit may be brought to maturity by storing in a closed paper bag at room temperature. Ripe fruit should be loosely covered and refrigerated. June and July are the peak season for apricots, although some imported fruit may be available in December and January.

AVOCADOS Many people forget that the avocado is a nutritious fruit and can be used effectively when making desserts. It is not sweet, but has a bland flavor and buttery texture that combines well with other ingredients.

The fruit should be heavy for its size and free of bruises. Avocados bruise easily. Skin color varies from light green to almost black, depending upon the variety. Size and texture of the skin also vary. The flesh of all varieties, however, looks and tastes similar.

Avocados ripen well once picked, and they are usually sold in a hard condition. To ripen fruit, store in a dry place at room temperature for a few days. They will yield to slight pressure when ready. Ripe fruit should be stored in the refrigerator. Once cut, the fruit must immediately be dipped into or sprinkled with lemon juice or ascorbic acid to prevent browning.

Avocados are grown primarily in California and Florida and are available all through the year, being especially plentiful from January through April.

BANANAS This one hundred percent imported fruit is in steady supply all year long. Unlike other fruits, bananas have the best flavor when picked green. Plumper bananas are usually of a higher quality than spindly or oddly shaped fruits. They should be held at room temperature until the skins are a full yellow color and flecked with brown dots. Many people, however, prefer this fruit on the firm side, when it still has a slight green tip or is all yellow, but without the brown flecking. Avoid fruit that is soft or mushy and any with big dark blemishes or mold on the skin. Ripe bananas should be stored in the refrigerator; the skin will turn black and won't look as beautiful, but the fruit will be fine as long as it remains firm. Peeled fruit must be treated with lemon juice to avoid browning.

BLACKBERRIES AND DEWBERRIES These berries are similar, and in their prime should be clean, bright and plump, with a rich, solid color. Unripe fruit will have green or off-color drupelets and adhering caps; old fruit looks dull, soft and leaky. Store loosely covered and unwashed in the refrigerator, and use as soon as possible. The season is generally May through August, with peak in June and July.

BLUEBERRIES Select berries of a generous size, as small berries are less apt to be sweet. Good-quality, ripe fruit should have a plump appearance and a solid, uniform blue color; some berries will have a natural waxy protective coating, depending on the variety. The berries should be dry and free of stems, leaves and mold. Overripe berries are dull in color, leaky and sometimes shriveled. Immature berries will not be fully colored. Blueberries should be stored unwashed and loosely covered in the refrigerator, where they will keep for up to 3 days, if fresh. The season is the same as for blackberries.

CANTALOUPES When the melon is ripe, the stem scar is slightly sunken. Do not depend on a softening at the stem end to indicate ripeness, because repeated pressure will produce this even on unripe melons. Fragrant melons that give off a pleasant perfume are ripe.

Melons should have a solid rind color and a symmetrical shape, and should be free of bruises. Yellowing of the rind indicates over-ripeness; soft, sunken areas, and mold or moisture at the stem end, are signs of decay. Hold ripe cantaloupes at room temperature for 2 or 3 days before serving; this extra time and warmth will make the melon softer and juicier. Some people also feel that melon has more flavor when served at room temperature but, if preferred, it can be refrigerated before serving. Melons are available all through the year, but they can often be disappointing. California melons and those harvested in the summer months are really the best, reaching their peak in June, July and August.

CASABAS This melon is usually ripened off the vine. Ripe melons have a rich, yellow-colored rind and yield to slight pressure at the stem end; casaba does not have a perfumed odor. Underripe melons are hard, with greenish-white areas. Dark, sunken areas indicate decay. Store at room temperature for a few days before refrigerating. Casabas are available from July through November, but the best melons are to be found at the peak season in September and October.

CHERRIES Depending on the variety, the color may be very dark, bright or light red. Good-quality fruit is plump, firm and free of scars. Underripe fruit is small, hard and poor in color. Old fruit is soft, leaky and dull in color, sometimes shriveled. The best method of choosing is the taste test. Store cherries unwashed and loosely covered in the refrigerator for up to 2 days. Cherries are available from May through July, with the best to be found in June.

COCONUTS Botanically this is not a nut, but a fruit, the kind we call a "drupe." Coconuts are available all through the year; the peak season is September through December. Choose coconuts that are heavy for their size and full of milk; you should be able to hear the liquid slosh around if you shake the coconut. Those without milk are spoiled and those with wet or moldy eyes indicate decay. Whole coconuts can be stored at room temperature for up to 2 months; once cracked open, however, they should be covered and refrigerated for no more than 1 week. For longer storage, grate the meat, cover with the coconut milk, and freeze.

CRENSHAWS Ripe melons have a slightly soft rind at the large end, a golden skin and a fragrant aroma. Soft, sunken areas indicate decay. They are available from July through October, but are at their best in August and September. Ripe melons should be stored in the refrigerator; once cut, they should be covered.

DATES Although it is difficult to distinguish by appearance, dates are available either fresh or dried. Fresh dates, often called "pressed dates," are sold in health-food stores and specialty shops. They are sun-dried and completely natural, containing no added sweeteners or chemicals. You might wonder why fresh dates are sun-dried for, indeed, this sounds contradictory! The fruit grows in heavy bunches from the tops of palm trees. The individual dates are attached to a central stem by numerous slender twigs. To facilitate picking, the main branch is cut from the tree. Since all the dates don't ripen at the same time, it is necessary to place the whole bunch in a dry location to mature. In this way, dates can be either sun-dried, ripened by artificial heat, or by carbon dioxide.

Fresh dates look smooth, shiny and plump, and vary in color from deep yellow to golden brown. Old dates have a shriveled skin and sometimes have sugar crystals on the surface. Fresh dates will keep indefinitely if stored covered in the refrigerator. The season for fresh dates runs from September through May with November being the peak month. However, because they keep well, they are available throughout the year. Dried dates are discussed in the Dried Fruit section of this book.

FIGS Fresh figs are extremely perishable and do not transport well, so it is difficult to find the best quality fruit unless you live near the growing area. Ripe figs should be plump and soft without being mushy. The size and color will depend upon the variety. Avoid fruit that is bruised or cracked, or that smells sour. Refrigerate ripe fruit, loosely covered, for no more than 1 to 2 days. Fresh figs from California are available from June through October, and in their prime during August, September and October.

GRAPEFRUIT This fruit may easily taste sour, so careful selection is a must. Pink fruit has a milder flavor. A ripe fruit should be firm, springy and heavy for its size. The thickness of the skin is of the utmost importance. Thin-skinned fruit will have better flavor and texture and the most juice. Color is not an indication of ripeness. Avoid fruit with soft, spongy thick skin or pointed ends. Mold or sour odor indicate decay. Grapefruits are tree-ripened and ready to eat when sold. Store them uncovered in the refrigerator for up to 2 weeks.

Grapefruits are available all through the year: Florida fruit from October through May; California-Arizona fruit from November through May. Texas fruit may be found from September through June. The best grapefruit is to be found from January through April; out-of-season fruit has been held in cold storage.

GRAPES This fruit does not ripen once picked. Select grapes that are plump, firm and highly colored, and use the taste test. The grapes should adhere to the stems and should not fall off when gently shaken. Avoid clusters that contain small, underdeveloped or shriveled grapes. Wetness and mold indicate decay. Store in the refrigerator for up to 5 days. Depending on the variety, grapes are available all through the year, but August is the best time for the sweet, seedless variety.

HONEYDEWS Large melons are usually better than small ones; choose those that have a solid creamy-colored rind, with ends that yield slightly under pressure. A ripe melon should also have a perfumed aroma. Immature fruit is hard and white to greenish-white in color. Dark, sunken areas indicate decay. For maximum flavor and texture, keep at room temperature, away from light, for 2 or 3 days. These melons also have more flavor if served at room temperature. Honeydews are available through most of the year; however, the best season is from June through October.

HONEYBALLS These are similar to honeydews, but they are small and round. Best season is from June to November.

KIWI FRUITS These are imported from New Zealand. The bright green flesh, white core and black seeds are all edible. When ripe, they are slightly soft. Hard fruit can be ripened at room temperature. Store uncovered in the refrigerator. Kiwis are available from June through March.

LITCHIS This delightful fruit is only available fresh for a few weeks from late June to early July, but it is worth seeking out. Litchis can usually be found in Chinese markets. They can be stored in the refrigerator for 2 or 3 weeks, so consider buying a good quantity if you ever get the opportunity.

MANDARINS See Tangerines.

MANGOES The skins are multicolored green, red and yellow. Mangoes are usually bought while quite firm and ripened to softness at room temperature. Avoid discolored fruit with skin marred by black or grey areas. When soft, refrigerate uncovered. Many varieties are available in various shapes, sizes and colors from April through August, with June as the peak month.

NECTARINES This fruit must be very mature when picked or it will be unsatisfactory. A red blush is not a sign of ripeness, but the fruit should have some flushed areas. Look for plump fruit that gives under slight pressure. Immature fruit is hard, with a greenish hue, and will not ripen properly. Mature fruit, although hard, will have good color and will soften if held at room temperature for a few days. Dullness and shriveling indicate overripeness. Avoid bruised fruit. Ripe fruit can be stored in the refrigerator for several days. The season runs from June through September, with peak in July and August. Imported fruit, available in January and February, is not as flavorful. Varieties that come to market in the early part of the domestic season tend to be smaller and freestone. The larger sizes that appear later are mostly clings. Nearly all nectarines grown in the U.S. come from California.

ORANGES The best-quality oranges are firm, heavy for their size, and have a fine-textured skin. Avoid fruit that is puffy, spongy or light in weight. As required by law, all fruit is picked mature and therefore color is not an indication of ripeness; green fruit is as ripe as golden fruit. Softness, mold, yellowing and an off-odor indicate decay. Oranges store well in a cool room or in the refrigerator for up to 2 weeks. Numerous varieties are available at different times, but the following types (with their prime seasons indicated) are highly recommended:

VALENCIAS, from Florida, February through June, and from California, late April through October—a prime juice orange.

CALIFORNIA NAVELS, November through May—excellent eating.

FLORIDA TEMPLES, late November through March—excellent eating.

JAFFA (Israel), mid-March through mid-May—excellent eating.

PAPAYAS Choose smooth fruit that is more yellow than green, and avoid any that is bruised or shriveled. Ripen at room temperature until soft to the touch and mostly yellow or orange in color. Overripe fruit is very soft with a sour odor. Store ripe fruit uncovered in the refrigerator for up to 5 days. Papayas are available all through the year, but at their best from January through April.

PEACHES Select only mature peaches when shopping, because this fruit will not increase in sweetness after it is picked. Mature fruit has a good creamy-white or full yellowish background color; no green should be visible at all. Blushing does not indicate ripeness. If possible, try to taste the fruit before buying a quantity; if it isn't sweet then, it will never be. Hard fruit, as long as it is mature, will ripen satisfactorily if it is kept at room temperature. When ripe, the fruit will yield under slight pressure and have a delicious "peach-y" aroma; it may then be refrigerated for up to 3 to 4 days. Avoid peaches that are greenish, bruised, shriveled (even slightly), or very soft.

Peaches are available from May through October, but the best time to buy is June through August; the prices are lower and the fruit is most flavorful. Since peaches are grown in at least 33 states, you may find the opportunity to buy them locally.

Tip: Depending on how you are going to use the peaches, be sure to note whether they are freestone or cling; the freestones can save a lot of preparation time and will look neater in many dishes. Peaches can easily be peeled by dipping them into boiling water for 30 seconds, then immediately plunging them into ice water; the skins can then easily be slipped off.

PEARS This is one of the few fruits that taste best if they are allowed to ripen *off* the tree. Ripen at room temperature. The fruit should be free of bruises and firm, not hard. Russeting is not a sign of ripeness. Ripe fruit gives off a perfumed odor and is soft at the base of the stem. Avoid misshapen, wilted or shriveled fruit. Brush cut pears with lemon juice to discourage browning.

The best pears come from the western states and are available as follows:

BARTLETT, August to November.

BOSC, October to February.

D'ANJOU, October to April.

COMICE, October to February.

NELLIS, October to May.

SECKEL, August to December.

Firmer pears, those that are just slightly underripe, are better for cooking or baking because they have a better chance of retaining their shape than fully ripe or soft pears.

PERSIAN MELONS These must be fully mature when harvested in order to be sweet; they will not ripen satisfactorily if picked too early. They have a green rind with a yellow tint and give under slight pressure when ripe. Apply the same methods as when

Calendar Guide to Fruit Seasons

● GENERALLY AVAILABLE
△ PEAK SEASON

	January	February	March	April	May	June	July	August	September	October	November	December
All Apples	●	●	●	●	●	●	●	●	△	△	△	●
Red Delicious	●	●	●	●	●				△	△	△	●
Golden Delicious	●	●	●	●	●	●				△	△	●
McIntosh	●	●	●	●	●					△	△	●
Cortland	●									△	△	●
York	●	●	●							△	△	●
Apricots	●					△	△					●
Avocados	△	△	△	△	●	●	●	●	●	●	●	●
Bananas	●	●	●	●	●	●	●	●	●	●	●	●
Blackberries						●	△	△	●			
Blueberries						●	△	△	●			
Cantaloupes	●	●	●	●		△	△	△	●	●	●	●
Casabas							●	●	△	△	●	
Cherries					●	△	●					
Coconuts	●	●	●	●	●	●	●	●	△	△	△	△
Crenshaws								●	△	△	●	
Dates	●	●	●	●	●				●	●	△	●
Figs						●	●	△	△	△		
Grapefruits	△	△	△	△	●	●	●	●	●	●	●	●
Grapes	●	●	●	●	●	●	●	△	△	△	△	●
Honeydews	●	●	●	●	●	△	△	△	△	△	●	●
Honeyballs							△	△	△	△	△	●
Kiwi Fruits	●	●	●			●	●	●	●	●	●	●
Litchi Nuts						△	△					
Mandarins	●										●	△

	January	February	March	April	May	June	July	August	September	October	November	December
Mangoes				•	•	△	•	•				
Nectarines						•	△	△	•			
Valencia Oranges		•	•	△	△	△	•	•	•	•		
California Navels	•	•	•	•	•						•	•
Florida Temples	•	•	•								•	•
Jaffa Oranges			•	•	•							
Papayas	△	△	△	△	•	•	•	•	•	•	•	△
Peaches						•	△	△	△	•	•	
Bartlett Pears								•	△	△	△	
Bosc Pears	•	•								△	△	△
D'Anjou Pears	•	•	•	•						△	△	△
Comice Pears	•	•								△	△	△
Nellis Pears	•	•	•	•	•					△	△	△
Seckel Pears								•	△	△	△	•
Persian Melons							•	△	△	•		
Persimmons										•	△	•
Pineapples	•	•	△	△	△	△	•	•	•	•	•	•
Plums						•	△	△	•			
Prunes								•	△	•		
Pomegranates										•	△	•
Raspberries						•	△	△	•	•	•	•
Strawberries	•	•	•	•	△	△	•	•	•	•	•	•
Tangerines	•										•	△
Watermelons						•	△	△	•			

choosing a cantaloupe. Persian melons are available from July through October, with August and September being the peak months.

PERSIMMONS This very sweet fruit should only be eaten when fully ripe. Then it is soft and plump, with a rich orangey color. Firm fruit may be ripened at room temperature. Overripe fruit is mushy, leaky and/or shriveled. Avoid fruit with spots or broken skin. The stem-cap should be attached. The skin is edible, but the fruit may easily be peeled by the same method recommended for peaches. Ripe persimmons are very perishable; refrigerate and consume as soon as possible. They are available October through December, with November being the peak month.

PINEAPPLES This fruit must be ripe when picked because it cannot get sweeter after being harvested. Color and odor are the best indications of ripeness. Ripe fruit has a deep yellow-orange color, flat eyes and a fragrant perfume. Deep green leaves that loosen easily with a quick tug also indicate ripeness. The skin should yield slightly under finger pressure. Fruit should be plump and heavy for its size. Immature fruit has pointed eyes that are poorly developed; the skin is dull and often yellow, and the fruit will never ripen satisfactorily once picked. Mold, moisture, dark areas around eyes or at base, and softness indicate decay. Although they may be available all year, the best time to buy pineapples is March through June.

PLUMS AND PRUNES Many varieties ranging in color from yellow, green, red and purple (blue) are available, but basically they fall into two types: those called plums are clingstone and those called prunes are freestone. In both cases the fruit must be well matured with good color when harvested, because it will not ripen properly once picked. Ripe fruit is plump, slightly soft at the tip, with full varietal color developed. For optimum flavor and texture, allow the fruit to soften further at room temperature for a few days. Immature fruit is hard, poor in color and sometimes shriveled. Overripe fruit is very soft and leaky. Brownish areas indicate sunburn and the flavor is likely to be insipid. Refrigerate ripe fruit in the vegetable crisper. Domestic plums are available from June through September with July and August as the peak month; fresh prunes are available from August into October with September being the peak. Some imported plums may be available from January through March, but these are not as flavorful. The freestone Italian prune is the best variety for cooking.

POMEGRANATES The spongy white membrane is often bitter, but the seeds with juicy red flesh are delightful. Large pomegranates are better than small ones; choose fruit that is heavy for its size with an unbroken skin. Avoid dried-out-looking fruit that shows signs of decay. Ripe fruit will keep for several days either at room temperature or in the refrigerator. Pomegranates are available from late September through November with the peak in October.

RASPBERRIES This is one of the most perishable of fruits and should be bought for immediate use only. Choose clean, rich, fully colored plump berries. Immature berries usually have caps attached and have some greenish cells. Overripe berries are very soft, limp and leaky. The berries are fragile and should not be washed until ready for use; they should be added last in any fresh fruit mixture because they soften rapidly in liquid. Raspberries may be found from May through November, but the best season is June and July.

STRAWBERRIES Choose bright, solid-red berries with caps attached. Avoid those with any green or white areas and any with bruises. Size depends on variety and is not an indication of flavor or quality. Do not wash or hull them until ready for use. Like raspberries, they are delicate and should be handled in the same way and consumed as soon as possible. Although raspberries from Florida, California and other states are available all through the year, the best season is May through June. Whenever possible, buy local berries, as they will be the freshest and have the most flavor.

TANGERINES AND MANDARINS This fruit is characterized by its easily peeled skin. The tangerine was actually developed from the mandarin orange, which is noted for this distinguished characteristic. Other orange varieties with loose skin also have mandarins as ancestors. When canned, these are called mandarins. Because the skin is loose, the fruit may therefore not feel firm, and puffiness is an accepted part of the normal appearance in many varieties. Choose fruit that is heavy for its size with full deep-orange color. Pale or greenish-colored fruits should be avoided. Very soft fruit with water soaked areas or mold should also be shunned. Most varieties are available from November through January, with December being the peak.

WATERMELONS Choose melons that are symmetrical, firm, of a good color for the variety, and those that have a *creamy yellowish* underside. Thumping a melon is not a reliable method of determining ripeness. Rather, try to coax your produce dealer into cutting out a small plug from a whole melon so that you can taste it. Underripe melons are very hard, with a white or pale green underside; these will never ripen satisfactorily. Old melons are dull and springy to the touch and may have dark, sunken spots. A flat, dry leathery spot at the blossom end indicates decay. When buying a cut melon, the flesh should look crisp, with a bright, rich color ranging from light pink to deep red, depending on the variety. The flesh should appear wet and shiny, but not soggy. Unlike other melons, watermelon does not benefit by being held at room temperature for a few days. Ripe melons may be refrigerated for up to 5 days. Melons can be found from June through September, but the best are available in July and August.

Wine Buying Guide

Cyprian Wines: The vineyards of Cyprus have been under cultivation for over 7,000 years. The climate of the country is such that the sun shines more than 300 days a year, and thus yields grapes very high in natural sugar content. Because of this, there is never a need to add sugar to Cyprian wines.

Commanderie St. John

Cyprus Dessert Wine

This wine is as originally made during the Crusades by the Knights Hospitaller of the Order of St. John of Jerusalem, from the vines of the Commanderie of Kolossi Castle, Cyprus.

Produced and Bottled by:—

KEO LD
LIMASSOL — CYPRUS

Commandaria is a legendary dessert wine that dates back to the Knights Hospitallers and Richard the Lion-Hearted. It is a rich, luscious, amber wine that tastes somewhat like cream sherry.

St. Panteleimon is a medium-sweet white wine.

Keo is one of the largest producers of Cyprus wines that are sold in this country. Both St. Panteleimon and Commanderie St. John, produced by Keo, should not be difficult to locate.

French wines are among the most famous in the world. Although "chaptalization" (page 14) is allowed when necessary, the wine laws are otherwise very strict and complicated.

No doubt the naturally sweet white wines from *Barsac* and *Sauternes*, both located in the Bordeaux district, rate among the finest. They never have sugar added but are always sweet because they are produced from 'botrytised' grapes (page 14). There are many chateaux in both areas, and it is not too difficult to find bottles priced under $7.00, although many are much more costly. They are classed as table wines, yet have a rich, honeylike

flavor that has been likened to the nectar of the gods. Never substitute an American Sauterne for a French Sauternes if you want the French flavor. These are totally different wines.

Food and Wines From France, Inc., 1350 Avenue of the Americas, New York, N.Y. 10019 publishes a wonderful free Correspondence Course on French Wines. It contains a bounty of useful information and is definitely worth writing for.

Germany's new wine laws went into effect in 1971 and these laws guarantee that no sugar can be added after fermentation in order to sweeten a wine. Sugar which may have been added in poor growing seasons for "chaptalization" (page 14) must always be completely converted into alcohol during fermentation. Fully fermented wines which may then require additional sweetening can be blended with other sweeter wines from the same area that have only been partially fermented (without being chaptalized). There is only one category of wine which may never be chaptalized, those labeled *Qualitätswein mit Prädikat*. These are of the highest quality and are produced in five styles, one of which will be indicated on the label:

> **Kabinett**—dry
> **Spätlese**—medium-dry
> **Auslese**—medium-sweet to sweet
> **Beerenauslese**—very sweet (and quite rare)
> **Trockenbeerenauslese**—totally luscious (very rare)

Wines that are simply labeled *Qualitätswein* (without the *mit Prädikat*) are very fruity and range from dry to medium-sweet. Some German wines may be of particular interest to dieters. Those labeled *Trocken* (dry) or *Halbtrocken* (semidry) have less residual sugar. A *Trocken* wine only contains between 4 and 9 grams per liter of residual sugar and has been approved by the German medical profession as being safe for diabetics. *Halbtrocken* wines never have more than 18 grams of residual sugar per liter.

Unfortunately, the sweeter wines in the *Prädikat* category are quite expensive and it would be very extravagant to use them in quantity for cooking. You may find the *Auslese* style at a fairly reasonable price and use it in a recipe that only requires a small amount of sweet wine, and then indulge yourself with the remainder after dinner. Wines in the *Qualitätswein* category are less costly, but also less sweet. The quality, flavor and dryness varies widely, but many may be used in recipes calling for a medium-sweet white wine. With few exceptions, German wines are white.

You may obtain additional information on German wines by writing to the German Wine Information Bureau, 99 Park Avenue, New York, N.Y. 10016.

Greece with its sun-poached islands has a climate that's particularly favorable to the growing of sweet luscious grapes, so that the wines never need added sugar. The sweet red Mavrodaphne, named after the grape variety, is perhaps the most well known wine in the dessert category. It is a fortified wine, and its alcohol content varies between 15% and 18%. Portlike in character, it is best served at room temperature. Many other sweet wines are produced in Greece, but they are not widely available throughout the United States. Depending upon where you live, you may be able to find some delightful examples by searching through your local wine shops.

Hungarian wines bring to mind the famous 'Tokay' (Tokaj), of which there are three types: *Szamorodni, Aszú,* and *Eszencia.* All are naturally sweet, and this is a basic provision of the Hungarian Wine Law—no sugar may ever be added to grape wines. In bad growing-seasons, wines are permitted to be improved (the alcoholic level increased) with the addition of grape must concentrate, but even then the process is strictly controlled by the National Institute for Qualification of Wine. In order to obtain the desired degree of sweetness, the use of must concentrate may also be permitted after fermentation, when necessary.

California Tokay, an American dessert wine, should never be confused with Hungarian Tokay. The only similarity that exists between these wines is in the name. They are totally different wines and the informed consumer should be aware of this.

Szamorodni wines from Hungary are labeled either 'sweet' or 'dry' in very clear lettering. The sweet Szamorodni is served as a white dessert wine, but is not fortified. The sweetness is due to the fact that in some years, botrytis cinerea (page 14) develops on a large quantity of the grapes in each cluster. The grapes that have developed the botrytis are called *aszú* berries. These berries are not selectively picked; the entire clusters containing both the affected and the unaffected grapes are crushed together, making a fragrant sweet wine that is most charming and distinctive.

Aszú wine is made by different methods. The aszú berries, from Furmint grapes, are individually picked during the harvest, or selected from a table and collected in small tubs called puttony. When the harvest is over, the aszú berries are crushed into a pulpy dough; the grapes that were not selected as aszú berries are crushed into wine. The next step is adding the aszú dough to the grape wine. Here, the puttony is used as a unit of measure. Depending on the number of puttonos of aszú dough added to a barrel of wine, you will find bottles labeled three, four, or five puttonos. The number of puttonos is always clearly indicated on Hungarian Aszú wine. All these Aszú wines are sweet and luscious, but it is obvious that the degree of sweetness is contingent upon the number of puttonos indicated on the label—the 5 puttonos Aszú will be the sweetest.

Eszencia is a wine that few people will ever see, let alone taste; it is extremely rare. When the aszú berries are stored in the puttonos waiting to be crushed into the dough, a small amount of juice leaks out from the weight of the grapes and collects in the bottom of the puttony. It is this pure juice that makes the incredible eszencia. A puttony has a capacity of 7-7½ gallons, and the aszú berries can only yield about 3 pints of eszencia at the most. The juice is so rich that it ranges between 40% and 60% sugar, and it takes years for even a small amont of this sugar to ferment into alcohol, never exceeding 8%. Unfortunately, only a few fortunate people will ever experience the opportunity of tasting this exceptional nectar.

Italy has the strictest wine laws of any country and they are rigidly enforced. Sugar may never be added to wine under any circumstance, and those wishing to avoid sugar can feel secure when making a selection from that country.

Marsala from Sicily is perhaps the most popular dessert wine. It is a fortified wine produced in dry and sweet varieties, as well as in

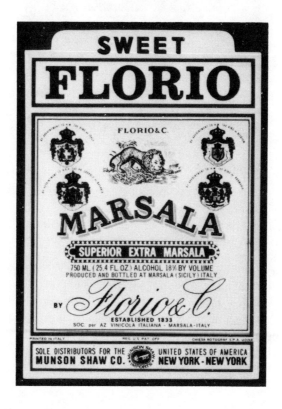

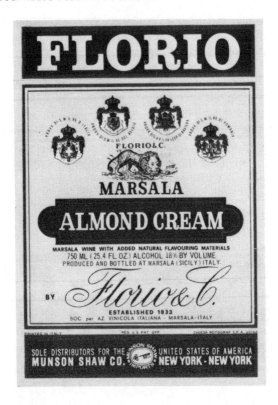

specially flavored versions—almond for example. An unflavored sweet Italian Marsala will be indicated by the words "sweet" or *abboccato* on the label. There are several brands on the market, but "Florio Sweet Marsala" and "Floria Almond Cream" are two favorites. They are both luscious and rich, yet reasonable in price.

Asti Spumante is one of the world's few sweet sparkling wines, if not the only one, that contains no added sugar whatsoever. The sweet, fruity flavor comes from the natural sugar found within the grape itself. In addition, the wine is low in alcohol, ranging between 7% and 8%. I highly recommend it.

Orvieto Abboccato from Umbria may be used in any recipe calling for a medium-sweet white wine. *Lambrusco* is a good medium-dry red wine.

NATURALLY FERMENTED

FRATELLI

CELLA

ASTI SPUMANTE

DENOMINAZIONE DI ORIGINE CONTROLLATA
ITALIAN SPARKLING WHITE WINE
PRODOTTO ED IMBOTTIGLIATO NELLA ZONA DI PRODUZIONE

CELLA

FRATELLI CELLA S.A.S.   SEDE MILANO—ITALIA

CASA FONDATA 1865

PRODUCED & BOTTLED BY G.M.N.T. ALBA-STAB. ASTI-ITALY
SOLE DISTRIBUTORS FOR THE U.S.A.-THE JOS. GARNEAU CO. NEW YORK N.Y.
NET CONTENTS: 1 PT. 10 FL. OZ.-ALCOHOL 8 % BY VOL.

Additional information on Italian wines may be obtained by writing to the Italian Wine Promotion Center, 1 World Trade Center, Suite 2057, New York, N.Y. 10048. A free *Italian Wine Guide* will be sent on request.

Madeira is a charming Portuguese island in the Atlantic, about 500 miles (800) km) southwest of Lisbon. It produces the famous fortified Madeira wines. Although none contain any refined sugar, they vary in degree of sweetness and it is necessary to read the label when choosing a bottle. One of the following types will always be indicated:

Sercial—dry, pale to golden in color
Verdelho—medium dry, golden
Rainwater—moderately sweet, golden, a blend of Sercial, Verdelho and/or Bual
Bual or **Boal**—medium sweet, amber, fragrant
Malmsey—sweet, dark brown, very fragrant

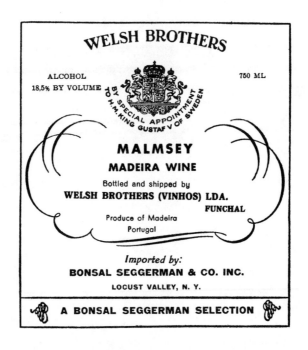

WELSH BROTHERS

ALCOHOL
18,5% BY VOLUME

750 ML

BY SPECIAL APPOINTMENT
TO H. M. KING GUSTAF V OF SWEDEN

MALMSEY

MADEIRA WINE

Bottled and shipped by
WELSH BROTHERS (VINHOS) LDA.
FUNCHAL

Produce of Madeira
Portugal

Imported by:
BONSAL SEGGERMAN & CO. INC.

LOCUST VALLEY, N. Y.

A BONSAL SEGGERMAN SELECTION

Portugal produces several noteworthy sweet fortified wines with Porto leading the list in popularity and availability. Several types of Porto (spelled with an "o" at the end when it comes from Portugal) are made, but *Ruby Porto* is perhaps the best candidate for our purposes. It is a fruity, bright, deep-red wine of young character. *Tawny Porto* is aged longer, which makes it a soft and elegant wine, paler in color, and it is slightly drier and less fruity than Ruby. *Vintage Porto* is all too rare and it would be an extravagance to use it in quantity for cooking. *White Porto*, although still sweet, is the driest of the Porto wines and as such is generally used as an apéritif rather than a dessert wine.

Moscatel de Setubal is another delightful fortified dessert wine produced in Portugal. It is now being imported into the United States by Frederick Wildman & Sons. Two styles are available, one is 6 years old and the other is aged 25 years in wood—both are golden wines.

Spain is divided into distinct wine-producing areas, each with its own traditions and customs. There is no national law that prohibits the addition of refined sugar in winemaking, but it is a practice that is frowned upon by the Spanish with their pride and strong sense of honor. Sweet grapes such as the Pedro Ximenez (often called PX), Muscat and Malvasia thrive in the hot, sunny climate, and it is their use in the sweeter wines that imparts the rich, luscious flavors.

Most of the sweeter Spanish wines that are available in the United States come from the Andalusian area, although it is justly well known for its dry wines. *Sherry* from Jerez is surely the most famous. It is a fortified wine produced classically from the Palomino grape in various styles ranging from very dry to sweet. The style is always indicated on the label:

> **Fino**—very dry, very pale
> **Amontillado**—dry, pale to light gold
> **Oloroso**—medium sweet, deep golden
> **Cream**—sweet, amber
> **Brown**—very sweet, dark brown

Additional information and free booklets on sherry may be obtained by writing to The Sherry Institute of Spain, 522 Fifth Avenue, New York, N.Y. 10036.

Sherries from California and other parts of the United States are generally not produced by the same method used in Spain. A few vintners, however, are producing some very fine sherry-style wines. See the section on California wines in this book.

Montilla, however, from the Montilla-Moriles district in Andalusia, is as true a sherry-style wine as is ever made. The differences in production methods are so minimal that Montilla looks, smells, and tastes just like sherry. It takes an expert to tell the difference. But, since it is produced in another zone, it is not allowed to be called by that name. It has the big advantage of costing less and it can be substituted in any recipe calling for sherry. Money-wise cooks would do well to remember its name. Like sherry, it comes in varying degrees of sweetness. *Montilla Oloroso* is medium-sweet, while *Montilla Cream* is sweet.

From Andalusia comes yet another naturally sweet wine called *Pedro Ximenez*. It is a dark, fortified wine that is very rich and

161

luscious, with a raisiny flavor. Alvear S.A. is one of the largest producers that supplies both Montilla and Pedro Ximenez wines. Pérez Barquero S.A. is a reliable producer of Pedro Ximenez.

The United States produces many admirable wines of its own. Many are named after famous foreign wines, such as Chablis, Burgundy, and Sauterne (the French is spelled with an "s" at the end). Most of these wines, however, taste so different from their namesakes that they cannot even be called imitations. While they can, indeed, be very fine wines, do not be misled by the similarity in name to the authentic product. Buy them for what they are, good American wines, not as substitutes for imported products. Should you choose to substitute, for example, an American sherry for a Spanish one, do it because you prefer the flavor. Today many imported wines may cost less than somewhat similar domestic ones, depending on the brand. But, the quality of the ingredients used in any recipe always speaks for itself.

California, by law, prohibits the addition of refined or artificial sugars to wine made from grapes. They may, however, be sweetened by the addition of grape juice or grape concentrates when necessary. There is a special provision in the law that excludes sparkling wines from this restriction.

In other parts of the United States, however, particularly in the eastern states, there is no law to stop producers from adding sugar syrups to sweeten wine, and many wines from these areas, though not all, are produced with such additions. Unfortunately, this kind of information is not provided on labels. This leads me to suggest that those who want to avoid refined sugars should stick to the products of California until such time as other states change their laws regarding this practice or require labels to contain such information.

Limiting selections to California, however, is nothing to grieve about, for some very excellent wines are produced there, and many are available throughout the United States. When searching out the sweeter table wines, be sure to read the label carefully. In some cases, producers indicate the percentage of residual sugar contained in the wine. One example is the 1978 *White Riesling* from Felton-Empire of San Luis Obispo. The alcohol content is low

—7½%—but the residual sugar content is high—12%. The wine itself is bright, fresh, fruity and luscious, and one can taste a hint of the delightful botrytis that graced the fruit from which this wine was made. As a general guide, a residual sugar content between 3% and 5% will indicate a medium-sweet wine, and anything over 5%, a sweet wine. The higher the percentage, the sweeter the wine. Only a few wines are labeled this way, however, and normally you will have to rely upon the descriptive literature also to be found on the label. The words 'sweet' or 'dessert wine' should be mentioned somewhere on the label if the residual sugar content is not.

1977
Mirassou
Fleuri Blanc ™

Monterey White Wine
Rich and Semi-sweet

Produced and Bottled by Mirassou Vineyards
San Jose, California · Est. 1854 · Alc. 12% by Vol.

In the California table wine category, you may wish to try:

Malvasia Bianca—sweet
Sweet Sauterne or **Haut Sauterne**—sweet
Muscat Canelli—sweet
Mirassou Fleuri Blanc—rich and quite sweet
Botrytis Sauvignon Blanc—sweet
Johannisberg Riesling, Late Harvest—sweet
Riesling, Johannisberg Riesling, or **White Riesling**—varies
Chenin Blanc—varies from medium-dry to medium-sweet
Sauvignon Blanc—varies
Semillion—varies
May Wine—medium-sweet, flavored with woodruff
Rosé Wines—vary, but usually medium-sweet
Late Harvest Zinfandel—sweet red wine

It is only natural that sweet table wines be called dessert wines. However, there is yet another class of wines in the dessert category—those that have been strengthened with the addition of grape alcohol (fortified):

Sherry: With a few exceptions, most are produced by special methods which are quite different from the Spanish.

In order to impart the characteristic nutty, sherry flavor, the wine is baked at a high temperature for several months. The best sherries are allowed to mature in oak casks, and this is usually indicated on the wine label. The style of American sherries are labeled:

> **Dry** or **Pale Sherry**—dry (up to 2.5% residual sugar)
> **Sherry** or **Medium Sherry**—medium dry to medium sweet (2.5% to 4% residual sugar)
> **Sweet, Golden, Cream,** or **Mellow Sherry**—sweet (over 4% residual sugar)

the

ChristianBrothers®

VINTNERS SINCE 1882

CALIFORNIA
CREAM SHERRY

PRODUCED AND BOTTLED BY THE CHRISTIAN BROTHERS
NAPA, CALIFORNIA, U.S.A. / ALCOHOL 18% BY VOLUME

The alcohol content of sherries ranges between 17% and 20%.

Port: Although these wines are made from different grapes, the style is very similar to the Portuguese Portos, and the wines are suitably labeled. Ruby Port may sometimes be called simply "Port." Residual sugar content of most California ports ranges between 8% and 10%. The alcohol content is not less than 18%. Ficklin is one vineyard that excels in making California port.

Fin de Nuit: This is a newcomer produced by Cresta Blanca Winery. It's a very distinctive sweet wine, made from a cream sherry base with an engaging combination of natural flavors added to it. The alcohol content of *Fin de Nuit* is 17½% and the residual sugar content is between 14% and 15%. It can be used in any recipe calling for a sweet sherry or even a sweet Marsala.

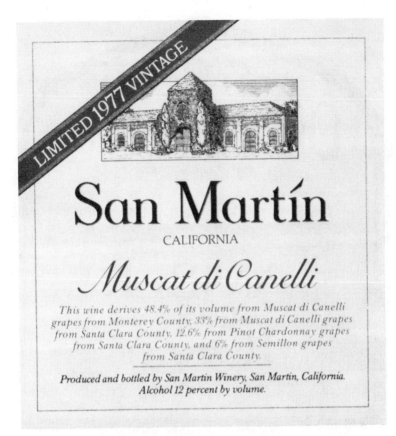

This wine derives 48.4% of its volume from Muscat di Canelli grapes from Monterey County, 33% from Muscat di Canelli grapes from Santa Clara County, 12.6% from Pinot Chardonnay grapes from Santa Clara County, and 6% from Semillon grapes from Santa Clara County.

Produced and bottled by San Martin Winery, San Martin, California.
Alcohol 12 percent by volume.

Other dessert wines are produced in California, but these are shunned by connoisseurs. They are so sweet that they cloy the palate. They taste flat and are tiring to drink. In addition, they have developed a sorry reputation—because they are inexpensive and come in small bottles, alcoholics with little to spend buy them as cheap substitutes for liquor. Nevertheless, none of these wines have sugar added to them; they are naturally sweet. In this respect you might find them suitable as a sugar substitute if used in moderation when cooking. In addition to being cheap, they are often sold in half-bottles, but they are not easy to find. You might wish to

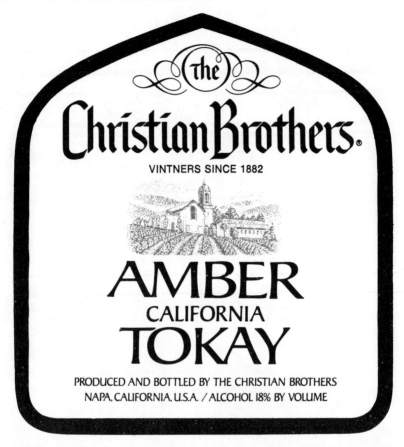

the

Christian Brothers®

VINTNERS SINCE 1882

AMBER
CALIFORNIA
TOKAY

PRODUCED AND BOTTLED BY THE CHRISTIAN BROTHERS
NAPA, CALIFORNIA, U.S.A. / ALCOHOL 18% BY VOLUME

experiment with these, if you locate them in a shop: *Angelica, Muscatel, Muscat, Aleatico,* and *Tokay.* Please remember not to confuse California *Tokay* with Hungarian *Tokay,* which is a very fine wine.

California *Madeira, Malaga,* and *Marsala* are poor imitations of the authentic imported wines. Availability has been rather limited since the trend for drier wine has taken over, but they're quite suitable for cooking, if you can find them.

Additional information and a free correspondence course on California wines may be obtained by request from the Wine Institute, 165 Post Street, San Francisco, California 94108.

SUGARED WINES AND SPIRITS

Champagne and sparkling wines from all over the world, including California, usually have a dosage of sugar syrup added before bottling, the amount varying with the desired sweetness of the final product. Such wines include *Champagne, Sekt, Cold Duck, Sparkling Burgundy, Pink Champagne, Sparkling Muscat, Sparkling Malvasia Bianca, Spumante* from California, and carbonated wines. *Asti Spumante* from Italy is an exception to this practice.

Kosher wines from all over the world and including the United States, although of high quality, are generally sweetened with the addition of sugar.

Fruit wines are those made from other than grapes. Only the grape contains sufficient sugar to carry out an unaided fermenta-

tion. In all other cases, including wines made from apples, apricots, berries, cherries, pears, plums, etc., it is necessary to add water and sugar to the vat. In some cases, however, the type of sugar added may be from fruit concentrates. Fruit wines from San Martin Vineyard in California are one example of those sweetened with concentrates, and you might wish to try them. They are sold under the label of the California Fruit & Berry Wine Company. With other brands, I would suggest that you write to the producer to find out what kind of sweetener has been used.

"Pop" wines, such as *Annie Green Springs, Bali Hai, Ripple, Thunderbird,* and *Wild Irish Rose* among others, fall into a special category called "natural wines." These, however, may be sweetened with sugar.

Liqueurs and cordials by law must contain a minimum of 2½% sugar by weight; many contain up to 35% of a sweetening agent.

Aperitif wines such as Vermouths are almost always sweetened.

There is no way to tell how any alcoholic beverage has been sweetened simply by looking at the label. Certainly there may be exceptions to the above. Should you be particularly fond of a certain product, you might wish to write to the producer directly in order to find out how it may have been sweetened.

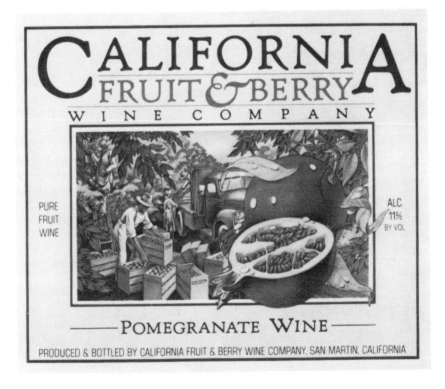

Bibliography

Abrahamson, E. M., and Pezet, A. W., *Body, Mind and Sugar,* New York, Avon Books, 1977, paperback

Duffy, William, *Sugar Blues,* New York, Warner Books, 1976, paperback

Grossman, Harold J., *Grossman's Guide to Wines, Beers, and Spirits*, revised by Harriet Lembeck, Charles Scribner's Sons, New York, 1977

Lichine, Alexis, *New Encyclopedia of Wines & Spirits*, Alfred A. Knopf, New York, 1977

Rhein, Reginald R., and Marion, Larry, *The Saccharin Controversy*, New York, Monarch Press, 1977, paperback

Rodale, J. I., *Food and Nutrition*, Penn., Rodale Books, Inc., 1966

Rosenthal, Sylvia, *Fresh Food*, Tree Communications, Inc., New York, 1978

Wile, Julius, *Frank Schoonmaker's Encyclopedia of Wine*, Hastings House, New York, 1978

Fresh Fruits, National Restaurant Assoc., Chicago, 1978, pamphlet

Nutrition Reviews' *Present Knowledge in Nutrition,* The Nutrition Foundation, New York, Washington, 1976

Dietary Fiber, United Fresh Fruit and Vegetable Assoc., Washington, D.C., 1976, pamphlet

Dietary Goals for the United States, United Fresh Fruit and Vegetable Assoc., Washington, D.C., 1978, pamphlet

Nutrition Notes 78, United Fresh Fruit and Vegetable Assoc., Washington, D.C., Winter 1979, pamphlet

Sugars in Nutrition, United Fresh Fruit and Vegetable Assoc., Washington, D.C., 1977, pamphlet

Supply Guide, United Fresh Fruit and Vegetable Assoc., Washington, D.C., 1978, pamphlet

You & Your Diet, "Exploding the Myths about Sugar," *Good Housekeeping* Magazine, 189:4, October 1979, pp. 176 and 178.

Index